SITES
UNSEEN

Carmen!
Look at the crazy
things I do. Enjoy!

Later

SITES

America As I See It

UNSEEN

LAURA E. WALKER

authorHOUSE®

AuthorHouse™
1663 Liberty Drive
Bloomington, IN 47403
www.authorhouse.com
Phone: 1-800-839-8640

First published by AuthorHouse   01/25/2012

ISBN: 978-1-4685-4798-6 (sc)
ISBN: 978-1-4685-4800-6 (hc)
ISBN: 978-1-4685-4799-3 (ebk)

Library of Congress Control Number: 2012901596

Printed in the United States of America

CONTENTS

Acknowledgements and Dedication

Not wanting to be overly schmaltzy, let me make a few quick mentions.

I know this sounds like one of those acceptance-type speeches, but I want to thank those who brought me into the world, and along the way once I was in it. You know who you are.

I'd also like to thank John-boy Walton. At age eight, I saw for the first time someone aspiring to become a writer. He inspired me to do the same.

I've got to give a shout out to my online patron saint of encouragement and a good idea. Kam, thanks for getting me to use what I got in the first place way back when.

As for my baby girl, I'm proud to be your Mama. Always remember, be brave, be bold, and be smart. How cool is that, you just read those words in my very own book! :)**B**

More than anyone else I want to thank Kim and dedicate this entire book effort to her. Your illustrations are awesome, or so I've been told. You got me going on this whole thing, telling me I should do it. Then you continually cheered me on and let me know I could do it, and now Sweets, we can both say together, "We did it!" Elephant Shoes.

INTRODUCTION

Welcome to Sites Unseen: America As I See It. Thank you for picking up my book and taking the time to read what I've got to say. I realize there are a whole lot of travel books to choose from, and a ton of inspirational tales of life-changing triumph, so your willingness to get in on this is something I really appreciate.

The main reason I wrote this book, other than to fulfill a lifelong dream of being published, is because I wanted to share my vision on living life. Give you my view on travelling. Or, how shall I say, get y'all to see things my way for a bit. I know that's a lot of visual referencing there, it's okay, blind people are allowed to say those kinds of words, as well as have them said to us. I thought if I start desensitizing you now, you'd start to loosen up, have a little fun reading at my expense, and maybe just maybe, you'd learn a thing or two. However, this isn't just a HOW-TO book; it's much more of an I-DID one. If you should somehow become inspired along the way, super and have at it. Honestly, you can never get enough of that kind of thing.

Now I feel it necessary to give you a little fair warning right up front; a disclaimer, so to speak. The contents of this book have been spell-checked to death. It has been thoroughly edited by a semi-retired English teacher, thanks again Jud B. Recommendations have been made considered, and, on the occasion, argued over. I say all this to let you the reader know, I am fully aware of my blatant bastardization of the English language. I knowingly will create words to convey my meaning, punctuate as I see fit, and misspell to emphasize a point. I am a rogue writer and refuse to be reigned. But if you catch a typo, just ignore it and we'll chalk it up to my blindness—thanks.

I'd like to say one more thing in this introduction section. Somewhere along the way of my writing Sites Unseen, I jotted down this phrase. *We, who are visionaries and use our mind's eye, have the advantage over those impaired with sight.* I don't usually go round claiming to be profound, but this really has it goin' on and pretty much sums up my personal creed. I may not be able to see too much in the physical sense of things, yet I think I'm sportin' 20/20 vision in a whole lot of other ways. If I've done this book right, maybe you'll be thinking the same by the end.

A LITTLE MORE ABOUT ME

Looking at the front cover, you have already learned a couple of things about me, from the most obvious being, my name, to my liberal use of word play. I have chosen this particular title for my book because I liked the gag. And just in case not everyone is in on it yet, I'll just say now for the record, I'm blind. Oh, the whispers begin. "Can she say that? Blind? Is that politically correct to say? I think she's got to use the word impaired, or visually differently abled, or something."

Well folks, I'm here to say it loud and clear, I'm blind and proud of it. You will hopefully pick up on my mindset that there's nothing "dis" about my ability. Oh sure, I have my moods where I'm less than fond of seeing everything like a giant smudge print on a camera lens with billions of mini flashing lights, but what's a girl gonna do. Let me back up just a smidge and fill you in on my formative years. This might help explain me better.

I grew up in a very white suburban neighborhood with two parents actually married, a younger sister helping me make up the 2.1 children in the household, and our grandfather living in the basement. Really, it was a very nice place for him, and we all lived quite happily there in New Jersey. My father went off to work every day and earned his living, and ours, as Associate Director of Athletics for Temple University in Philadelphia. My mother was the consummate housewife who could throw out an incredible spread of food whether it was holiday or picnic related. She was also President of the Marlton Garden Club two terms running, the first to have done so. My sister, Lisa, and I had an assortment of friends, a pool in the backyard, and the woods behind the house that we disappeared into for hours. It was all good and very normal, except for the fact that it wasn't completely.

You see, my eye problems were detected back in second grade with one of those simple school eye exams. A quick trip to the ophthalmologist led to years of visits with specialists. Throughout my childhood I had varying degrees of vision, all dependent on what surgery was performed in which summer. Now many may think, "oh how terrible for this poor little going blind girl," but honest, it wasn't really that bad. I was incredibly fortunate. I had a family that loved me, supported me in every thing I wanted to do, and sent my ass all over the place to do really cool things. I was usually gone up to the mountains or down to the shore for weeks at a time during the summer, to special camps for the blind and visually impaired. I got to compete in athletic competitions which had me flying or my mother driving me all over the place. I even was chosen to be an exchange student to represent the New Jersey Commission for the Blind and went to Scotland for three weeks.

I had so many advantages from my lousy eyesight that it didn't seem to matter. My lack of sight even got me out of vacuuming the pool and other vision deemed chores. It was great.

I've told you about all the awesome opportunities I had as a child growing up, now to the influences. I mentioned my father's job. In holding this position, he had to travel with the various teams to some incredible destinations, like New Orleans, Hawaii, and Tokyo, Japan a mere eleven times. My mother was able to accompany him on many of these trips and I always remembered thinking a couple of things as they packed their bags, "Why can't I go with them?" And, "I'm gonna go there someday."

Another tremendous influence would be my maternal grandparents. They are one of the true American stories, for they immigrated to the United States by boat in 1952, with my mother in tow. They lived their lives well, holding to the German work ethic, a strong sense of family, and made wonderful friends along the way. My grandparents always were involved in everything we did, and when they weren't, they were off somewhere traveling. I remember them going to visit family back in Germany numerous times, heading to California to see the Rose Parade, traveling the eastern seaboard and eventually making it to Nova Scotia. In their later years, Florida was the winter haven of choice. My grandmother so much wanted to go to Branson, Missouri for the shows. She booked a trip package and headed off on her own regardless of her some seventy year status.

Opportunities and influences certainly factored into my being who I am, but I don't want to over look my own personality. I have an innate curiosity that has led me to seeking, learning, and doing. Barring my teen years, I have a generally low threshold for most forms of embarrassment, and will try just about anything despite how ridiculous it or I may look. My tendency to be less than shy has served me well too. I thoroughly enjoy learning about other people, cultures, and I love history and learning the origins of this or that. I wouldn't refer to myself as brave just foolish enough to go ahead and do. Maybe more importantly than any of these traits, is my ability to trust. No matter how independent a person might be, at some point or another there will be the need to trust in something. Whether it's another person, the weather, or in a higher power, trust is a necessity.

I have told you about my life up to a point, yet there is one very important piece I must explain from my recent past. Even though my life has been great, it hasn't always been easy. I am no super hero with dynamic abilities to thwart the villains of blindness. I've struggled, gotten angry, cried, and all that "woe's me" stuff that helps a body into a place of acceptance. Generally, it was never my diminished vision that held me back; it inevitably was the result of my lacking my own internal strength, faith, and confidence.

So when the new millennium rolled around, my sight waned into little more than seeing through soup and fog at the same time. All the doctors and their band aids weren't working anymore. My eyes finally said "enough is enough". I'll be honest, there were several life alterations all happening at the same time, and the least of my worries then were being blind. I almost felt relief because the struggle to see was exhausting, both physically and mentally. But it took time to realize it, along with a good therapist, friends and family supporting me-oh, and let's not forget the Prozac.

In time, I found myself again. All that cool and good stuff I mentioned before, came bounding back stronger than ever. Hell, I hardly get embarrassed anymore, and I adopted the mindset of a two year old. "If I can't see them, they can't see me." It works very well for me. With confidence abounding, I soon realized I had given up some of the things I loved doing. Among them would be travel and writing. I made a promise to myself in the year 2001 and began my own odyssey of having one amazing trip experience each year.

I've held to that promise and have even expanded on it. I typically take a couple of trips a year now and attempt to have at least one of them on foreign soil. Those particular experiences will hopefully lead to another book, but let's just concentrate on this one for now. I decided to write about a few of my American travels first because in some way or another, everyone can relate. Possibly it's because of a visit in person to Chicago, or having watched the television show "Friends" and feeling as though you've been living in New York. Maybe it's from studying the history of our country and seeng all those pictures of Boston. Or perhaps San Francisco seems familiar due to a movie viewed like Disney's "Princess Diary" and Alfred Hitchcock's "Vertigo". Whatever association you may or may not have with any of these incredible places, I was privileged to wander into, I hope you enjoy reading what happened to me, and those daring enough to go along for the ride.

ABOUT MY COMPANIONS

I'll say this right up front. I live a truly blessed life. My adventurous spirit, generally un-shy ways, and ability to see beyond the obvious are all some of the parts which make the whole of me. These are qualities I deeply appreciate, but it's the blessings that make me grateful. With your permission, I would like to name them one by one; for they are the wonderful women I have in my life, who were there for the adventures.

The following cast of womenly characters will appear soon enough in the book, but I thought a little getting to know them was in order. Please note the order of introductions is not based on favoritism, alphabetical standing, or length of time known. Rather, my arbitrary decision of who was crazy enough to spend the most time with me got top billing. You may also want to revisit them before reading their corresponding city section, just as a refresher. So with no further adieu, the lovely women of Sites Unseen.

Kim Shepard

Kim is probably the most courageous of all the women you will meet. I can say this because not only did she make everyone of these trips with me, but she shares the daily adventure of my life as my partner. She's learned the "joys" of living with me and survived the innumerable ways I inevitably draw attention. Subtle I am not. This all speaks to her own abilities to adapt, but I want to let you know of her innate attributes as well. Kim is a beautiful person, both inside and out, who has an incredibly loving and generous heart. She is willing and wanting to try new things and travel, but is ever the cautious one making sure daring does not replace sensibility. Kim will read every placard offered, is unable to pass a map by without thorough inspection, and will snap a picture of any sign she fancies. Appreciation is apparent as her sweet, big brown's light up when she laughs, spends time with family and friends, or sees the cuteness of a youngster. Beauty being found in the beholder's eye, Kim's wonderment has her seeing it all over the place. I love her, and lucky for me, she dittos the sentiment.

City Appearances: All of 'em.

BOSTON

Sarah Mitchell

Understanding and wise beyond her years is my sweet baby girl, Sarah. And yet, she is the total incarnation of today's teen types. Here is an example of both. Sarah was a mere seven year old when my eyes went their final way. Grasping the concept of blindness, she adapted to things on her own. Disappearing for a while, she converted the picture she had drawn to a tactile rendering by using up most of the Elmer's glue to outline her work. When it had dried, she presented the weighty art to me and said, "Now Mommy, you can feel what I drew for you." Gets you right there doesn't it? As for the other side of Sarah, she has the selective hearing capacity of any teenager. She will text message all the live long day if permitted, and as for her room, I'm just not going to let myself get started on that. Sarah possesses a sensitive and kind heart. She is aware beyond her own wants and feelings, and often shows a maturity that just freaks me out. She has grown physically over the course of times traveled, leading me to move my hand from her shoulder to her elbow when being guided. Sarah has a beautiful soul, and I am overwhelmed with pride and the honor of being her mother.

City Appearances: New York City, San Francisco, and Chicago.

Doris Walker

I'll sum my mother up by saying, "she's one hell of a classy broad." Everything I'm not in terms of proprieties, dress, decorum and other such things, she just drips with. Statuesque and graceful, my mother is truly a dame. Of the British variety that is, not the "South Pacific" version. Although she made the ultimate journey as a small child immigrating to America, and has subsequently been many places accompanying my father on business trips, my mother has been somewhat reluctant to take her tuchus on the road of late. However, when asked to keep an open mind to join us, she overcame her natural tendencies, and did so. Oh the lengths and miles a woman will go to spend a little quality time with her family. For a momentary stroll into seriousness, I'd like to share; my mother has always been there for me, even when it wasn't easy for her. She was there in those days of endless hours sitting in eye doctor offices or hospital rooms after eye surgery and on into the here and now with my loving Kim. She may not have planned my life exactly this way, but she has always let me pursue my life as I saw fit and had made clear she loves me. And that's why, people, I call her Doris Walker Superstar!

City Appearances: San Francisco.

Judy Benson

I've said it a thousand times before, and I'll say it a million more, Jud B rocks! The energy and enthusiasm with which this woman approaches life, and certainly any project, is phenomenal. I delight in her very distinct personality, "aw-shucks" mannerisms, and use of the English language. Having now coined the term, Jud B-isms, I would define it as, "the use and crafting of words into phrases uniquely uttered by the one and only." An early riser, long john wearing in the middle of summer and all around swell gal, Jud B. has found a special little niche in my heart. I have learned a lot from her no nonsense approach to life. Yet I realize a softer, sensitive self exists under the dynamo exterior. And on the occasion when it peeks out, I like it too. Yes Jud B, you do rock, in so many ways.

City Appearance: Chicago.

Nancy Thrams

If I were limited to a few words to describe Nancy, some of them would be; she is a born leader, likes to tote her nut filled tea water around with her, and is a woman of conviction and opinion. Fortunately though, no such limitations are placed upon me at this time, so let me rave on a bit about this amazing person. I love being with this woman who takes the time to enjoy the simple smallnesses of life, recognizing the importance of each. Nancy's youthful heart, seeking soul, and unwavering tenacity to live and acquire knowledge are just some of the reasons I admire her so. Her curiosity regarding my blindness is completely endearing, and because of this, and the fact she is rather fond of me I believe, she is often the first person to offer her "wing" to guide me. The word profound gets thrown around a lot, but it is most accurate when used to describe Nancy's spiritual self. I am often challenged, in the best possible sense, by Nancy's beliefs and ideas to examine and discern my own. I could quite literally stop right now and do a happy dance as I think about our friendship, its growth, mutual admiration, and joy felt from having Nancy in my life.

City Appearance: Chicago.

Fran Twomey

I would describe my good friend Frannie as one of the most natural people you'll ever come across. She has this beautiful ease about her, the wonderful gift of humor, and an insatiable need to know guised as curiosity. The Frannie "Huh" conveys through its airy lilt, her sense of wonder, disbelief, or simply a thought provoked. Her good natured demeanor and down to earth interactions are something to behold, because Frannie approaches everyone as an equal. I've observed her unassuming self chatting it up with all sorts of folks, and can't help but smile as her warm spirit catches others, drawing them into a feel good moment. As personable as Frannie is, she is also as personal. I remember once telling her I thought she was an enigma, which of course elicited the Frannie response. Looking it up later to make sure I was using the word correctly, which I was, I soon realized I was confusing my own wanting to know her better, with Frannie's private self. Thing is, it was a catalyst of sorts. Frannie has greatly enriched my life, and I am deeply grateful to have such a splendid friendship with her.

City Appearance: Chicago.

Vicki Miller

Take equal parts raw energy, extreme generosity, a brain that knows something about everything, and mix it all up with a perky disposition, and right there you'd have Vic. This woman is either one of the most giving persons I know, or she's simply an insane glutton for making her own life difficult. All this will become clearer when you read later of our one day foray, but as for explaining just how good a person this little lady is, I'll try to make sense of this. When I see people my way, I often forego giving them a face, or at least the features upon one. Instead, I turn the feeling I get from the individual into an image. When I see Vic, I see a big, pearly white smile. I also see summertime, because I've been told she's got the blue eyed blonde thing going on which adds to her bright personality. So there you have it, the very essence of Vicki is sunshine and a smile. A body can't help but feel good hanging with Vic, and any chance I get to, I'll always take it.

City Appearance: New York City

There you have it, my blessings and the best travel companions a girl could ask for. I'd hit the road again in a heart beat with any one of them. Reading on, you may want to take a moment to re-acquaint yourself with my gal pals who all have made my life so much fuller just by knowing them. It's my hope our shared experiences will provide a chuckle or two, maybe some inspiration or at least a good read.

1

BOSTON, MASSACHUSETTS

It was once said," There's no place like home." I think this sweet sentimental belief system of the home body is kinda true, but when the traveling bug sinks his teeth into me, look out. My ever tolerant partner, Kim, has lived this truth all too frequently with me over the years. The internal itch to wander is easily triggered in my case with such things as a sunny day luring me out and about. Simple airline ads have left me wanting. And television alone has baited my curiosity into a feverish need to be elsewhere.

The dis-ease that grows within me to stay put has led me to endlessly suggest a variety of destinations. I've been shot down more times than I'll ever admit because of such ridiculous reasons as responsibilities, money, and time. But on the occasion, the moon and stars align and Kim agrees we should go. Such was the case with a long Labor Day weekend and cheap airfares leading us to a great get-away to Boston. And thanks to the last-minuteness of our decision, nary a lick of significant planning was done with the exception of a quick peek online to check out how a couple of gad-abouts would do just that.

Before I get all up and into what happened to us in Boston, I thought I'd take a moment and give y'all a few need to knows about the place. Boston is a great place to visit, but I wouldn't want to drive there. Notorious for its decade spanning road construction project, humorlessly referred to as "The Big Dig," getting about within the city is best left for the veteranned and strong of nerve. That left Kim and I out by a long shot. Option B quickly became the public transit system, commonly known as "The T." The idea of taking this means of movement was to keep our costs down, and allow us easy access to places we wanted to visit.

Obviously, and most famously, Boston is known for its instrumental role in the beginnings of our American ways. Our beloved country's united and stated history got its very start thanks to a few rabble rousing boys. Historical perspective has later bestowed these fellows with a more prestigious naming of the Founding Fathers. We all learned in school about the acts of protest perpetrated by those daring revolutioners, from the Boston Tea Party, to those far more conspiratorial and stealthy rides over the lands where Mr. Paul Revere declared the British to be coming. These actions of defiance and determination have significantly contributed to the passion for freedom and justice held in this country.

Not to be out done by the fore fathers, a few more upstarts laid claim to history when the Boston Red Sox broke an 86 year slump and won Major League Baseball's World Series in 2004. Unbelieved it could ever be done, they did so, and turned city, state, and world on its ear with their incredible triumph. Maybe not so much for me and the Cleveland Indians fans that year, but anything had to be better than those damn Yankees winning again. Putting aside rivalry for an evening, it seemed a jaunt to the famed Fenway Park and taking in a game would immerse Kim and I in the Bostonian culture of our current era.

Destination decided and paid for, Kim and I readied ourselves for the fun to be, and the interesting learning awaiting in Boston. But we had to get there first.

NOTHIN'S EVER EASY

Beginnings of vacations and trips can be very telling, and ours to Boston would have told us plenty, if we could've heard it. Yet hearing that small inner voice is nearly impossible when panic is screaming out ever so loudly. Foreshadowing may be evident when reading a book, but life doesn't seem to provide these kinds of conveniences. I'm not for certain, but maybe it's best this way.

Our Boston trip called for us to be up well before the crack of dawn. I'm not normally a willing participant of early morning wake-ups; however my ever scheming thought process went something like this. If we got there by mid-day it would practically count as the whole day, and we'd really make it a long weekend. So a little strategic planning was done to ease the earliness factor. Kim has friends living just minutes from the airport from which we were to fly. Such a convenience could not be ignored, and led to an over night invite. One I encouraged Kim to initiate.

Arrangements made, we sauntered into our host's home the evening before our flight, and spent a bit of time visiting. Kim and I earnestly insisted our hosts not fuss over us, all we required were clean sheets and a toilet. We were interjecting ourselves into their routine, and we didn't want to disrupt any more than we already were. But as hosts do, they did provide friendly conversation, a guiding of where the breakfast goodies were, and we were shown to our room when it was time to say goodnight.

Not wanting to disturb these kind people anymore than we had, Kim and I set the clock for 3:30AM, placed the ticker under our pillows, and pounced at its annoying alarm awakening us. The expression may be about time flying when having fun, but I gotta tell you, it's even quicker when asleep. I also feel the need to mention that tip-toeing around someone else's house I don't know is not such a treat. Those objects that are somehow easily avoided when the senses are more alert and oriented seem to place themselves right in my path at this time of the morning. It never seems to fail when I'm half asleep the sudden excruciating pain of a toe stubbed or a shin banged against a piece of furniture is just the catalyst to full awakening. This morning was no different. As I quietly worked my way down the hall to the bathroom, rearranging the pictures hanging on the walls with my groping fingers, I soon found a chair or maybe a bookcase; I don't know what it was except it hurt. I swear it wasn't there before we went to bed. And as I swore to this, I swore at it too, all the while gritting my teeth and stifling my own self.

The rest of the house experience was fortunately uneventful and far less painful for me. Kim and I gathered our overnight gear, played follow the leader down the stairs, and wrote a note of thanks as we exited. Part of our preparations for this trip was to secure reliable directions from one place to another. Let me tell you, just because those online mapping suggesters say go thata way, or signs appear for an airport, doesn't mean it's necessarily what is wanted. I'm not sure when would be a good time to learn this lesson, but I can guarantee you, it's not in the wee hours of the morning as one is trying to catch a flight.

Up and down the highway we went, our speed ever increasing, along with the volume of our voices. Kim and I are truly loving partners, except when it comes to directions. She reads them. We get lost. I get angry. It always progresses this way no matter how hard we try to avoid it. Our relaxing ride slid into a mild case of anxiety, then a state of panic. At some point in utter frustration Kim crumpled and threw the betraying online instructions into the backseat. We were deranged people in a strange land simply seeking a way out.

Not knowing where we were or even which way to go, we did the only thing we could. We woke up our hosts with a phone call to ask for directions. So much for not making a nuisance of ourselves, but we had no choice as that nice check-in cushion slipped away. Kim kept a tight grip on the steering wheel as I conveyed our host's instructions to her. Over hill and dale we flew through the darkness. Tension and frustration still reigned supreme, however with a witness on the other end of the phone line; Kim and I were forced to behave better.

Soon a sign appeared in the distance. We held our collective breaths as our Toyota Corolla's high beams illuminated it. Stark white letters cut the darkness and spelled out words of hope and joy, Akron-Canton airport. Never in the history of all mankind have any two people, three if you count our weary navigator on the other end of the mobile, rejoiced so gratefully in seeing a sign. Even though we drove the 25 minute ride to the airport in a record breaking hour and ten minutes, we felt the thrill of victory.

We barreled our way into the long term parking lot, Kim barely using the brake with the little to no time we had remaining. I have always lived up to my naming of Walker, never wanting to exceed this pace. But on this blackened morning of hurry, I set my speed to giddy-up. Bursting through the terminal doors, we hurriedly managed the check in counter. The complete desperation of a flight leaving without us was being felt by us both, especially when told we had only fifteen minutes to get to the gate. Kim and I scurried as rapidly as possible to and through the security screening, which was the only thing going our way this morning. Kim grabbed her possessions and began the time consuming luxury of replacing her footwear. Getting as far as almost one shoe completely on, I interrupted with, "there's no time for that!"

Our mad dash to the plane resumed as we ran hell bent on making it. Kim teeter-tottered as she one shoedly clip-clopped across the concourse, with me holding on to her for dear life in my slippery socked feet. Hitting the designated gate at full throttle, Kim and I careened along the entry ramp much like Olympic lugers and boarded the plane. Our appearance was nothing less than a spectacle, as our sweaty, huffing, toting sneakers in hand selves, clambered down the narrow aisle to our seats. All the while we were praising Jesus, the universe, and anyone else listening, for getting us there on time.

The brief flight to Boston barely left time to recuperate from the morning's mayhem. Nerves frayed and needing settled, I gave serious consideration to ordering a stiff drink but decided against it since it wasn't even seven o'clock yet. A short flight goes something like this. Doors are shut, the plane is catapulted into the sky, beverages are served while still in a state of ascent, garbage is collected exactly three minutes later, then seat backs and tray tables are restored to their proper positioning as the plane descends from the approximate fifty feet it had been flying at. Mind you, I might be exaggerating here, but I assure you; it's minimally.

The arrival into Logan Airport went suspiciously well. Kim and I agreed to forgo checking luggage and do the three day trip with only the packs on our back. Our thinking—we wouldn't have to wait around at the luggage claim, and waste valuable site seeing time. Brilliant—and to our surprise it actually worked. So if anyone reading this is keeping track, that's one good idea that succeeded and 1 that nearly led to our emotional and physical demise.

Luggage claim ignored, we found our way out to the airport shuttle service, and the T. Boston's subway system was what we figured on using to get us to our hotel. Our sleep deprived harried hungry selves approached the T entrance hoping to find a friendly Bostonian who'd help us with directions. Instead we met up with written instructions, the need for exact change, and a ticket producing machine that summarily refused us. I tell you, the hounds of hell were far more accommodating than this blasted thing.

Raw nerves inched us both closer to the edge, but somehow we maintained some semblance of control. I'll never know what the difference was between the first and tenth try to get one of those golden tickets, but when it was finally released to us, we celebrated our triumph right through the turnstile. The underground labyrinth of this color line and that passageway had me convinced a Minotaur would be leaping out from a darkened corner at any second. To be honest, I wouldn't have minded either, just as long as he was willing to point us in the right direction. Instead what we met up with in those subterranean tunnels was a number of local citizens eager to impart their knowledge. Thing is, they didn't have a clue either. Oh, we got directions, got some place, but not necessarily where we wanted to be. I'll admit, all subways look the same to me, but c'mon you people who see and proclaim to know what you're talking about, give a couple of visitors a break.

Kim and I back tracked, hell we even side tracked to end up on some corner of Copley Square. We knew we were close now, and this gave us the strength to carry on. Like a choice really existed there. Looking for our hotel, the John Hancock became an exercise of idiotic proportion. It seems not only the below ground travelers could be errant in providing instructions. I stopped listening to anyone who started their advice with, "I think you go . . ." Even Kim's fervent need to verify everything by looking at any and all maps along the way never had us being where we wanted.

The whole thing got under my skin. Nothing made a difference, and I let my complaint be heard loud and clear. So when Kim told me there was a map just ahead, I stopped dead in my tracks and proclaimed, "I'm not taking another step!" Unphased by my declaration and probably glad to be rid of me for a little while, Kim went on to check out that map. She even kept going a bit asking another person, and did finally end up finding our hotel. Me, well I was all alone in making my stand. I was still clueless as to where I was, and now I'd gone and lost Kim. Abandonment issues and annoyance had surpassed into downright piss-offedness. Thoughts coursed through my brain such as, "I can't believe she just left me here . . . doesn't she know I'm blind?" Cell phone calls I urgently made went unanswered and I became grossly indifferent to the lunatic appearance I exhibited when screaming for Kim as loudly as I could down the open streets of Boston.

I heard nothing more than the loose autumn leaves scattering about my feet in response. No Kim. No call. Just me standing God knows where because I sure didn't. A car or two drove right on by completely oblivious to my dire solitary state. I waited as angry, quite censorable tirades coursed through my mind. So when Kim finally did come back, I wasn't sure what to feel, relief, or like I was gonna give her such a smack with my stick. I held my tongue. I think partly for fear of what ugliness would come out and mostly, because my teeth were clenched tightly together.

I was seeing red. Not a lick of rational thought was left within me. Not even the slightest chance of understanding my responsibility in all this remotely remained. Previously I've mentioned having the mindset of a two year old, in that if I couldn't see you, you must not be able to see me either. This is usually one of my self perceived virtues and keeps me from worrying about my appearance, but right now, it wasn't so much. I needed some kind of censor, something to make me shut up. The only thing that held true at this point for me was "out of sight, out of mind." Kim was out of sight, and I became quite out of my mind.

It might've looked like I was calmly holding onto Kim's elbow outwardly, but inwardly I was stomping my feet and having a good ol' flailing fit. I held it together for a couple of blocks, but as we crossed yet another street and Kim guaranteed the hotel to be "right over there"; I couldn't hold it back any longer. KABOOM! The muzzle came off and out it all spewed. Everything from the idiocy of our early morning near miss of the plane, the incomprehensible stupidity of people in general, to, "Why the hell didn't you answer your cell phone" came out. Not so secretly I was holding Kim accountable for each and every mishap we encountered. And for some reason, she'd have none of it. Kim was all up in my face just as much as I was in hers. It was like we were possessed and a sort of exorcism was taking place in us both. We let loose the demons of travel misconnections, misdirection, and miserableness.

God knows who witnessed our incensed gesticulations and utterances, but fortunately no one saw fit to involve law enforcement. Even though words were exchanged angrily, Kim and I do somehow know where the line exists, and never have crossed it in terms of making it irreparable. We both needed to let off steam, and really, what better convenience than a place where absolutely nobody knows you, and you'll never run into them again. The ugliness stopped and our minds rightly returned. Sincere apologies were exchanged and accepted by each as we moved away from the street corner. Funny thing is, as Kim promised, the hotel that she assured was right over there, really was.

LAUGHING ALL THE WAY

One spit bath, two granola bars, and a few moments lying down restored our minds and will to go on. I'm not kidding either, because we both considered holing up in the hotel room after our harrowing morning. But a little recuperation goes a long way, and it was time to pound some Boston pavement and locate the tour bus we had decided to use.

Kim and I were neither stupid nor daring enough to rent a car and deal with city traffic, even worse, the parking. So we picked one of those get on get off guided bus tours. For those of you who may not be familiar, these things have designated boarding spots on a mapped route around the city. The rider has the option to stay on and listen to a tour guide impart their knowledge all the way round. Or, one can disembark at those spots, visit a bit, and then re-board to hear yet another guide. A tour guide can make or break any experience no matter how wonderful the sites being seen are. This may be even truer for me since I'm the one depending on the narrative play by play. Little things like accurate and interesting facts should be a given since that's what the guides are there for, but a pleasant personality, good delivery and a sense of humor, can turn a drab history lesson on wheels to an entertaining educational experience.

Our decision to use the Old Town Trolley tours was based on two factors. One, the vehicle was not in the shape of a giant rubber ducky that when approaching water, actually converted into a boat. We agreed, A non-cruising land tour was more our speed. Somehow the idea of looking ridiculous never really entered into it. And the second selling point, one of those hop on spots was conveniently right around the corner from our hotel.

Kim and I packed up a couple of essentials and strode out the hotel front door with an air of confidence. We were leaving the driving to someone else; all we had to do was find the pick-up point. To my utter astonishment and overwhelming joy, we found . . . Dunkin Donuts! You people don't understand. I love donuts. I've said it plenty of times; I'd marry ice cream and have an affair with a donut. Fortunately Kim is not threatened by my love for my sweets. Seeing, or more accurately stated, smelling my beloved right there represented not only a later rendezvous, but a good omen. It was as if the gods of gluttony were smiling down on us, assuring us all would be well from now on in Boston.

The gods were right, for only a few steps further stood the Old Town Trolley sign post. Also, the wait wasn't long before a bus showed up. Kim and I presented our pre-printed online tickets and met the first of many local characters. I'm thinking Boston is endowed with a high populace of these types, because we sure met a lot as we trollied about the city. One driver after another edu-tained us with relevant information delivered as an amusing bit. For example, Mr. Baseball told us Harvard's scholarly history while citing all the ways the Red Sox were the best team in the game ever, backing everything up with pre-recorded sound effects. Kim and my personal favorite though, totally cracked us up. It was like taking in a stand-up show. She got great audience participation when she taught the Boston dialect by holding up flashcards with the proper pronunciation and spelling. We outta towners learned quickly by repeating after her, "Don't evah pahk ya cah in Hahvahd Yahd."

As good as a tour guiding bus driver may be, it's the company you keep that can often be a deal breaker. I'm not speaking of Kim of course; rather it's those strange riders sitting alongside you. Think about it; what if they smell badly, or gurgle when they breathe. I certainly have had my fair share of unpleasant persons sitting near or next to me. Now I'm about to tell you something I never thought I'd say in my entire life. If you can swing a city visit while an Elk Convention is there, do it. Give me a second here to explain myself.

You know some old gals, especially the social ones, like to gather together. Sometimes it's a church thing, for others it might be some kind of club. When a club is the local chapter of a whole big national organization, the over powering need to migrate and meet up is an urge that can't be resisted. I don't know for certain exactly what they all do when convened, but WOO WEE those old gals know how to have a good time on a bus. Our first encounter with some of these ladies of leisure went something like this.

Kim and I innocently stood curb side waiting for the trolley. Her eye caught the rolling red vehicle approaching before my ear did, but it was me who heard the raucous sounds of a good time as it pulled to a stop. The doors hissed opened and just like a Jack in the box, the driver popped her head in the doorway and said, "Welcome to this wild ride!" Never one to shun a potential good time, I urged Kim up and on into the fray. I don't think I'm over stating it at all when I say; it was love at first laugh.

Not unlike Marlin Perkins of Mutual of Omaha's Wild Kingdom, Kim and I carefully entered the Elkettes natural habitat. They were spread out all over the place, clearly marking their territory with the shopping bag trophies of previous conquests. Kim and I slipped in among them, trying not to disturb the banter. Completely captivated by their rowdy charm, we observed the Elkette dynamics in action.

In such a group as this, there is always at least one who stands out a bit more than the rest. If for no other reason than sheer volume, cutting through the already loud din, I could hear the boisterous and ever so distinctive laugh of one lady Elk. Her gravelly guffaws let it be known, I am woman, hear me roar, with laughter that is. The naming choice of this generation emphasized utility over perkiness. This means the chances of one of these gals having the name Marge, Alma, or something along these lines are very high. My assumption made, was proved when I heard someone call out to Maude from across the bus. This particular flock of lady Elks, or would it be herd, had no problem cracking wise. Any bone of shyness had long since submerged beneath a few extra pounds of good dining. They certainly weren't afraid to share an opinion or laugh out loud either, and did so about everything. Their comments went from the seats being too hard, to the occasioned driving tip offered, as well as providing additional color commentary on history itself. I know they weren't actually around when it was being made, but I'm not so sure they didn't.

We were easily the youngest by decades on that bus, but fitting in didn't seem to be a problem. We quickly became one of the gals when a tune naming trivia game was initiated by the driver. Kim and I knew each song and singer, and yelled out the answers, but we didn't stand a chance of being heard over the aged bobbysoxers. I couldn't keep myself from laughing right out loud when some song from the fabulous 40's was played and in unison, the girls would blurt out, "Frank Sinatra . . . Bing Crosby . . . Deano!" I swear I heard them still swooning for the crooners after all these years. Then when the answers were confirmed as correct, they'd commence to cackling about how wonderful those singers were and they don't make songs like that anymore.

Mixing it up a bit, the driver threw in something a little more current, like Chuck Berry's Maybellene. The gals were completely dumb founded into silence. I knew the tune, but for the life of me couldn't come up with the dude singing it. It was only Kim, the youth of this America, who had the answer and let it be known. I don't know this happened for sure, but it felt as if the whole bunch of them did one of those double takes at Kim. I don't think they were expecting such an assertive answer out of this sweet faced young lady. Thing is, Kim didn't say her answer louder than she had been doing all along. It was just their silence and her enthusiasm that made this one a little more noticeable. As sudden as Kim's answer was, so were their response of applause and atta-girl shouts.

Had we stayed on with the lady Elks any longer, I think junior membership would've been in our near future. We were having a blast with our gal pals. So much so that Kim and I seriously considered staying put and riding the rest of the way with them. Those Boston sites had been there a long time, and weren't going anywhere is kinda how we figured it. But in the end we decided to stick with the original game plan and made way to the exit. Reminiscent of one of those movie scenes at a train station, we stood on the sidewalk waving our adieus as the trolley pulled away. The whole rip roarin' gang of'em replied in kind, "Bye, Good-bye!" And off they went rolling loudly away, still laughing. So if you don't take anything else away from this book, I want you to at least remember this one thing. If historical touring ain't entertaining enough for ya, go the hysterical route with the Ladies, Elkettes that is.

THE FREEDOM TRAIL

Boston is clearly aware that their big draw for visitors is its significant role in American history. And like any self-respecting capitalistic society, you are obligated, nay, I say, ordained to capitalize on what you got. It's the American way. Thusly, tourist traps are born. Amidst all the historically preserved places you'll find the essentials. Souvenir shops, re-enactors, themed eateries, and the like. Together they work to create a wonderful milieu for visitors to spend their money, which in turn, keeps the economic circle of life thriving.

Ease and accessibility are essential lynch pins when it comes to how the American tourist will make vacation decisions. This is not to say we're a lazy lot, instead rather, and generally speaking, most of the star spangled set lives are complicated enough. When we get away, we don't want to fret with any potential difficulties. The good folks of Boston's tourism industry know this, and have designed the Freedom Trail to accommodate those easy needs. A self-guided tour of Sixteen of Boston's most historical sites along a marked walking path is available.

Boston may have built an industry based on its past, but it was the here and now Kim and I were going to venture through.

Our mission, locate the visitor center and get the goods on where to go. What a brilliant concept, make information accessible about all the wonderful things to see and do in one centrally located place. Free literature, maps, and people knowledgeable regarding the this and thats folks want to visit. A visitor center is a nifty invention and incredibly handy, when open that is. Unfortunately for us though, the blasted thing was closed. We were left standing there asking ourselves "why us" amongst a myriad of other such ponderances.

Plans thwarted, we were forced to improvise a solution. Rather than re-enacting our own revolting battle from earlier in the day, we simply decided to have a go at the Freedom Trail on our own. This was yet another chance for me to practice blind faith, the obvious reason need not be stated further, but for Kim, this was a whole new experience. The woman had no map. The closed visitor center left her visually impaired, of the overall area that is. We had to trust we were just as capable of doing what thousands of other tourists do every year.

Finding the red bricked Freedom Trail next to the Visitor's Center was a piece of cake, and led to the next decision, which way to go. Without a map we had no way of knowing what lay where, so despite our liberal leaning tendencies, we went right. The beauty of the day naturally conveyed itself to me as I felt the autumn sun warming my skin. The light breezes rattled the remaining leaves upon the trees as Kim and I casually strolled along. Over the years of our being together, Kim has learned and become a great setter of scenes. Her visual dependence really works in my favor, because the gal takes it all in and can't stop herself from sharing. This symbiotic relationship of her having someone listen to her excited utterances and my seeing things through her eyes is just one of the many ways we are compatible.

As we strode along the trail's way, I began to notice a pattern in Kim's descriptions. Inextricably mixed in on itself were the past and the present. My preconceived notion of the Freedom Trail leading us to one historical site after another was completely wrong. I should've

13

figured that everyday life would be in and among, but when I heard Kim describe a colonial building with a Honda parked out front and interfering with her photo shot, I realized just how intertwined past and present were.

We had been walking for some time and were seeing sites, but not exactly the historical ones we wanted. Unanswered questions abounded. "Where's Paul Revere's house?" "Shouldn't we have seen something by now?" "Do you think you can find a bathroom?" All pertinent to our situation, yet nothing was forthcoming. Questioning and walking, we crossed over yet another street and suddenly, it was gone. No Freedom Trail anywhere in sight. No more red bricks. Not even the red paint that filled in on occasion. The whole kit and caboodle appeared to have been dug up and replaced by a construction project.

Kim and I began reviewing our options. Turn around, circumnavigate the bulldozed area and hope to find something on the other side, or simply call a cab and make it a day. Quitters we're not, and forward thinking a virtue, we decided going on was the best thing to do. Kim deftly negotiated us through the bad lands of the construction, telling me to step over this, duck here, and assisting me in negotiating between a fence-like barrier type contraption. Sure, most people would have taken the hint of neon orange warning signs and bright yellow restrictive tape, and kept out, but not us.

Seen safely through the rubble, Kim landed us on the other side and found, absolutely nothing. The elusive red marked Freedom Trail remained unseen. I don't know how we do it, but we seem to have more than our fair share of ending up in the middle of nowhere, even when nowhere is surrounded by a city. I'm telling you, calling a cab was beginning to sound pretty good right about now. We didn't really want to turn around either, but without a map or some kind of signage we were beginning to wonder if this was the end of the trail for us.

Then all of a sudden and without warning, there were people everywhere around us. Okay, it was only three of them, but with this whole not seeing thing, it feels like people magically pop into my life. Thing is, they were standing there all along, I just didn't know it. From my point of view, they never even existed until they startled me with "hellos". These unexpected strangers mirrored our very own situation of the trail vanishing on them. An instant camaraderie was formed when we realized we were coming at the same problem from opposite sides. Reassurances were exchanged, along with a few directional hints, and we sent each other off to the sort of more known. I'm pretty sure Kim and I got the better end of the information exchange, especially since we only knew where the closed visitor's center was. They in turn happened to have an extra tour map and generously gave it to my gleeful gal who clutched the treasured artifact to her bosom as she repeatedly expressed her gratitude.

As advised, we took this turn and that, cut through a small outdoor market, and somehow stumbled back upon the red trail. Map in hand and red underfoot, we finally found our first official Freedom Trail site. A really old cemetery with a bunch of dead revolutionaries was buried there. Under normal circumstances Kim and I might've been fascinated with the names and dates carved into the headstones, yet the effort already exerted in finding this relieved us of any real curiosity. Cursory glances given, a few names read, we re-engaged the trail to locate its saving grace, the Old North Church.

Old North was on my bucket list from the get-go. Its white steeple jutting into the blue sky is indelibly pictured by my mind's eye. It will forever be indebted to Henry Wadsworth Longfellow's poetic phrasing, "Oneth by land, and twoeth by sea." This poem immortalized the lantern signal used to warn outlying revolutioners of the manner in which the King's army would advance. Because of the Old North Church's part in the American Revolution, many historically inquisitive folks have sojourned to its doors. That's them, now me.

I'd like to say I learned of this American sacred site because of educational studies, and show off the good public school system efforts in learnin' me, but I cannot. For in truth I must confess it was, Sears! Yep, a number of years back Sears had a commercial for their outdoor paint and the Old North Church was featured. The slogan went something like this, American landmarks are entrusted with our stuff, so it's gotta be good enough for you. I'm paraphrasing here.

I'm begging y'all right now, whatever you do; please don't tell Miss Krauss, my 8th grade history teacher, that I was inspired to seek this site because of a commercial and not from what she taught. That no fooling around, trench coat wearing, German named teacher was one tough educator. Truth be told though, I began my love for anything historical in her class. I even learned the Constitution's preamble for extra credit even though my grades didn't require the support, at least in this class. I remember reciting it to Miss Krauss and trying my darndest to keep from sing songing it, since School House Rock was my tutor.

My limited vision still has the ability to see white, and white I did see as we approached the Old North Church. Kim and I wandered around the building's outside first so I could get a feel for its size. Making way to the front doors, I stopped and looked upward, straining both my neck and eyes to try and see the steeple outline against the sky. Although my mind's eye presents a far clearer picture, the real deal eyes came through and barely made out the blurry blob stretching towards the heavens. It was right there and then when all the hassle of the day became worth it. Excited energy coursed through me as I rushed Kim inside. I've always noticed no matter what sacred structure a body enters, a certain hush falls over the person when there. And so it was for Kim and me as she whispered the scene to me. I listened to her intently as she described the simple altar space, the use of stained glass, and read to me various inscribed plaques. I felt the old wooden floor beneath my feet give a creak slightly as I ran my hands over the pews. I thought of those who worshipped in this space, whether it was the some two hundred years before, or those still gathering today. I then created in my mind the darkness needed for those men who lit and shone the lantern from the steeple above and wondered if their hearts raced then as quickly as mine did now.

I loved being there and taking it in. All my senses were on full alert, minus taste of course. I wasn't about to lick up some history for Pete sake, but soak it up, I surely did. As if that weren't enough, the most exciting discovery came from a simple flyer Kim glimpsed in the entryway of the Old North Church, telling of a one man oration on Paul Revere. Whether it's called spontaneity, impulsivity, or decisiveness, doesn't really matter, because the results can turn out the same. We agreed to take the chance and come back later; figuring the story telling potential would be tremendous.

Our trail experience certainly was not a smooth one. In theory the Freedom Trail is a really cool idea. Practically speaking though, it sucked. We did eventually manage to come across some of the touted sites of the Freedom Trail thanks to the bus tour we were using. The following are some literal snapshots of the few we did have a chance to visit.

Quincy Market

Once a trading and farmer's market littered with livestock and produce, it's now crawling with tourists. At least the theme of shopping hasn't gone away over the years. Today you'd be hard pressed to find yourself a sheep, but wooly sweaters and socks, they got. Corn on the cob can be found as those teeny little cute corns they put in Chinese food. And the days of schlepping through muck and mire of mud has long since been replaced by the convenience of a brick walkway. The market is also home to the replicated Cheers bar and a worthwhile stop if you're a fan of the show.

Faneuil Hall

Home and meeting place to the Sons of Liberty, our founding forefathers who fought for freedom. It remains a public gathering place, the second floor designated to be used as such, while the first houses shopping opportunities. To be completely honest, had this not been directly in our path to get into the Cheers set, I don't know if it would have been worth the stop. I guess a selling point could be, it did have a tiny post office which allowed us to actually mail our postcards in the city we were in rather than from home.

Bunker Hill Memorial Monument

Fashioned after the Washington Monument, this memorial commemorates the valiant battle between the revolting colonists against the Britt's. Wait a minute, revolting as in fighting against, not gross or disgusting like, and they were all Britt's back then, so let's say the King's army. The entire battle consisted of three waves of advancement by old King George's boys, and over the course of three hours. The rag tag rebels were technically defeated, however since the paid British army sustained so many casualties, it was regarded as a victory of sorts and bolstered the revolution along. If you want to see a great model depicting the entire battle of Bunker Hill, the memorial's museum houses a really neat replica. One worth seeing but not touching since it was under glass.

Paul Revere's Home

At least one of the ones he lived in during his eighty-three years on this earth. Although best known for being Mr. Revere's residence, it will always be known to Kim and I as the "Where the hell is it?" house. First of all, who'd believe it would be smack dab in the middle of Boston's Little Italy, and then tucked ever so discreetly behind bricked walls with nothing but a tiny sign to declare its presence. Needless to say, this wasn't one of our more easily found establishments. However it was interesting to learn a bit more about the person behind the patriot, and how folks lived back in the revolutionary era.

The USS Constitution

Also known as Old Irons Sides, not to be confused with the wheelchair bound lawyer of the 70's series bearing the same name, rather, this was the first commissioned ship of the American Revolution and navy. The nickname came about due to the British navy's inability to sink her, as they themselves lost ships when engaged in a battle upon the seas. Apparently the weapons of mass destruction from back in the day, cannons and their balls, appeared to have no effect. The shock and awe placed upon the now swimming Brit sailors gave way to the utterance, "Surely, its sides must be made of iron." Our own visit upon this ship was ever so brief thanks to time constraints and waning energy levels.

AN EVENING WITH PAUL REVERE

Our bodies had accrued a tremendous amount of wear and tear on this first day in Boston, so I felt a reward of sorts was needed. Oh sure a hot soak could've been the easy answer. Simply taking off my sneakers and airing out my feet would've been okay. But what my body yearned for more than anything else were donuts. Oh those powdered sugar covered creamed filled marvels from Dunkin Donuts had never left my thoughts since we had first discovered the shop practically attached to our hotel. Now nestled atop our bed with bag in hand, I pulled out number one of two bakery offerings.

I sat there with the heavenly confectionary held between my fingers, and ever so carefully, I sniffed its delicious aroma. Slowly and gently I touched my tongue to the donuts rounded exterior and began the dance, seeking out the cream hole opening. I had learned in my youth, eating from the wrong side could result in a catastrophic loss of the white delight. A mistake I vowed would never occur again. Mingled sweetness and anticipation created an explosion within my mouth. I swallowed hard to contain my mouth's excited response. Finally, it was there on the tip of my probing tongue. A creamery dollop burst forth from its baked doughy self. I needed no better an invitation than this. I inhaled slowly, not wanting to disturb any loose powder. My breath caught and I moved in for that first glorious bite. Unadulterated rapture took place within my mouth. Oh how I succumbed to the joy over taking me and moaned my pleasure. My donut gave itself to me, fully and freely, as I captured it over and over, until there was no more.

Satiated, I collapsed back onto the bed, completely spent. Kim, who was occupying her own self in the room, turned to me and simply said, "Was it good for you?" My gluttonous reply, "You have no idea how good." As I said before, thank goodness she's not the jealous kind.

I was drifting in and out of a sugar coma, when Kim decided it was time to get going. We had a date night with Mr. Paul Revere and neither of us wanted to be late. Assuring ourselves safe passage there, Kim and I hailed a cab to take us back to the Old North Church. We planned on arriving early enough to stake out some good seats, and with so few in attendance, we didn't have a problem finding any. Pews for the picking, we headed straight for the front pew box and tucked ourselves in, closing the little door behind us.

Corralled in and trying to get comfortable on the mercilessly hard wooden bench was quite the feat. The unforgiving stiff seat was not what our 21st century posterior parts were accustomed to. This has consequently led to my new found appreciation of pew pads.

For those of you unfamiliar with a pew box, allow me to do some explaining. Nearer to the front of Old North are these high walled contained pew sections. These cubicles served a couple of purposes, of which I will address—practicality and functionality first. Given the northerly location of Boston and its place upon the harbor, the winters are known for its brutality when it comes to cold. Central heating not yet an option in 1723 when the church was built, another means was needed to keep the congregation from freezing. Hot coals and bricks were brought in and placed on the floor of the pew boxes, where the heat would be better contained by the high surrounding walls. As for those poor common folks in the back of the church without this arrangement, I imagine they just huddled together and shivered a lot.

This then leads to the other purpose of these preferred pews; the seats denoted a place of standing within the community. The boxed symbols of status belonged quite literally to the elite who paid handsomely to brandish their names upon this place of distinction. The more the contribution, the better the location, and the closer to God they'd go. Our benefactor of front pew seating was one Captain William Maxwell, who probably would've been none too happy with our first come first sit takeover of his spot.

Fidgeting with anticipation and in an effort to find a comfortable position with which to sit, I waited like a hyper active child for the show to begin. I tell you, I truly believe Kim should receive some kind of saint status when our life gig is up, how she puts up with my endless questioning I'll never know. From the basic "what's this?" to the more specific burning need to knows that pop into my head, the woman has grown accustomed to my peppering pleas for information of the visual variety. Her rescue came by way of dimming lights and the polite applause of the small audience welcoming Mr. Revere to the forefront.

David Connor's portrayal of Paul Revere is utterly convincing thanks to his striking resemblance to the early American activist, or so I've been told. But it's his keen story telling in the first person that sucked me right in. In a conversational manner, Mr. Connor shared the amazing life of Revere, his influence, and his participation in the American Revolution. Taking his uncanny look-alike self, he has developed quite a career depicting the revolutionary hero in a variety of settings, such as the A&E television show Biography, in the museum home where the man himself once lived, and here at the Old North Church.

I became completely captivated by the man's assuming manner, believing Paul Revere was truly speaking to us and sharing interesting tidbits of his life. How the man had time to father sixteen children as he plotted and planned a revolution is beyond me, yet he managed to squeeze it in along with his well-established silver smithing business. I already knew of his midnight ride alerting the countryside of the eminent on coming of the King's army, but I was completely unaware he had participated in the Boston Tea Party dump. An active and influential member of the Sons of Liberty, Mr. Revere aided and abetted this conspiring group of freedom seekers by any and all means available to him.

I was so engrossed by this wonderful depiction I was virtually able to ignore the numbing sensation of my buttocks, my attention remaining riveted on every word. I felt as if he, the actor and the man, was speaking directly to me and responded in kind. Catching my surprised reaction to the law preventing women from ownership of any sort, the Mr. Reveres incorporated my disbelief and addressed me directly with the 1700's reasoning. In rapt fascination I listened to his historical accounts weave into a story of a man, the beginning of a movement, and was taken by word and imagination to the founding of our nation. It was truly an awesome travel back to the beginning of our country.

I could've easily turned a brief meet and greet after the performance into a full out Q&A discussion session with the man. Unsure whether he would remain in character, or if I should refer to him as Mr. Revere or Connor, couldn't, and didn't, stop me from asking questions and sharing my enthusiasm. The gentleman, whatever persona stood before me, was gracious in welcoming my delighted inquiries. I whole heartedly recommend if you should trip into Boston, see if the wonderful opportunity to spend an evening with Mr. Revere exists, and take it. It's utterly worth the while.

CHEERS TO THE CHAMPS

There are many good things about securing passage on a pre-decided tour, and I could probably extol some of those virtues right now, but since it has absolutely nothing to do with where I'm going, I'll just hold off. Rather, there's much to be said for living in the moment, letting the wind carry you where it may, and taking opportunity's advantage. So went this second evening in Boston, when Kim and I went along for the wonderful ride.

Our quintessential Boston evening began with the one, the only, Cheers. Thing is, there's really two of them though. The iconic sitcom making Sammy, Norm, Cliff, Carla, and all the rest household names and answers to trivia questions, harkened its likeness from a small Boston bar by the name of The Bull and Finch. Randomly picked from the phone book, the Cheer's creators approached the pub owner to snap a few shots, leading to the immortalization of his bar and the reason for our visit.

Watch almost any Cheers episode and you'll see the exterior of the now well-known Bull and Finch. Kim and I hiked a mighty long way to get to this spot and once there, turned into the typical tourists. Snapping pictures of each other in front of the bar, walking down the outer stairs, in the doorway, we well chronicled our step into television history, while simultaneously exhibiting our nerdiness. And for the record, I am quite an able photographer, as long as my subject is willing to play a quick game of Marco Polo with me. The invention of digital cameras have further enhanced my abilities, for with film it was always point and pray, hoping to capture the intended shot. Now I can shoot, re-adjust a smidge if needed, and score the perfect photo.

Walking into the Bull and Finch Kim and I stood atop the same type of platform steps found on the television show's set. And according to Kim's report, all similarities ended right there. I cannot speak for those who have made the pilgrimage over the years to these hallowed grounds, anticipating Norm's corner bar stool, or anything reminiscent of the beloved program, only to be bitterly disappointed in the nots. Not a stool, a wooden Indian, a single feeling of familiarity was present; nothing we've come to associate with Cheers. No longer wishing to upset the public or wanting to explain for the millionth time the exterior shot scenario, and possibly recognizing a really good business opportunity, the original owner of the Bull and Finch created a replica of the beloved Cheers set in the heart of Quincy Market. Kim and I went to both of course, yet the almost-be is where we sat this night.

It's ridiculous how excited a body can get just being in a place you feel you already know. But I guess that's what happens when a TV show is allowed into your home for so many years. The perk of blindness came into full view as my mind's eye overcame the reality of the Bull and Finch setting, and squarely placed me in the Cheer's bar. Kim and I poured over the menu and ordered up a delicious bowl of genuine New England clam chowder, a couple of screaming Vikings to wash it down, and some cleverly named burger, which I can't remember for the life of me. I'm thinking the Viking possibly had something to do with my memory removal. Even though nobody there knew our names, it didn't diminish the experience one little bit, because visiting a cultural pop icon is always a good time, especially as I see it.

Satisfied with having visited our must-stop spot, Kim and I climbed the stairs leading back up to street level and realized the night was still young. Ideas of what to do were bantered about until decision was made to saunter on foot to Boston's famed Fenway Park. The walk along Beacon and Commonwealth allowed some more site seeing for Kim, who delighted in all the old fancy Bostonian homes and the liberal use of wrought iron. Having secured directions and assurances the walk would take us no more than half an hour, at the fifty minute mark we began having our doubts the place even existed, much less believing it was nearby. As darkness fell upon us, and all seemed most bleak, a heavenly sign appeared unto us. Thank God for the blimp hovering over the ball field!

It took'em 86 years to break the curse, but the Boston Red Sox did just that when they won the 2004 World Series. Giving them bragging rights for the entire 2005 season, BoSox fans have been partying ever since—and why the hell not. Personally, I've partied over far less. It was a perfect night for baseball. We got all caught up in the moment and followed an impulsive itch to take in a game. This was impossible to resist, especially being a Cleveland fan. It's not too often we get to see a World Champion team play. Plus the added attraction of Fenway, the oldest ballpark in these here States. Did you know that Fenway's opening day took place April 12, 1912? A rather infamous day if you were cruising on the Titanic.

Red Sox fans milled about eating, drinking, and whatever elsing all over the streets leading up to the stadium. We could hear the distant echoed voice of the PA announcer sounding not unlike one of the Charlie Brown adults. Knowing something was being said, but not sure what, we could only hear "Waa wa wa waaa wah," followed by the roar of the crowd.

The energy was electric as we approached the stadium; amid all the sounds I could hear the scalpers hard at work. It was a night of chances and thrills, so we approached one industrious gentleman to acquire a couple of seats. Not wanting to appear as some rube, I inquired, "Are these real tickets?" I've heard the stories and wasn't gonna fall prey to some disreputable scalper. His reply of guarantee came as this, the kindly fellow stretched his arms wide and said, "There would be no honor in stealing from you." I guess if there's honor among thieves, there's gotta be some among scalpers. Either way, I was in, and we bought two tickets for the bleachers.

Kim and I passed through the turnstiles entering Fenway just as the home team smacked one out of the park. Frenetic fans are something to witness, so we quickly scurried our way even further into the stadium to see the going ons. Tunneling closer to the field, we avoided the wrong turn at Albuquerque, and popped up right behind home plate.

Bleachers my Aunt Fanny, it was time for the sighted one to put those baby browns to good use and scan us up some seats. And boy, did she ever. Kim located two on the aisle about twenty-some rows back. Badah-boom badah-bing, there we were, two Cleveland gals livin' like baseball royalty. It wasn't long before we struck up a conversation with the gents behind us. It seems asking people to take a picture usually leads into that sort of thing, at least for us. They knew those seats didn't belong to us, especially since the previous occupants had just left minutes before, but they knew we were harmless, not to mention kind of cute, so they let us stay. Not like the semi-drunken dude that had just tried the same thing prior to us and got the boot.

I knew only three things about Fenway Park before going, and they were: it's the oldest ball park in the country, it's the home of the Red Sox, and a Green Monster lurks in the outfield. Since then I've learned some fun facts about Fenway that I hope to edu-tain you with now. That Green Monster I spoke of is the affectionate nickname bestowed on the left field wall, which obtained its envious color back in 1947. Standing thirty-seven and a smidge feet tall, it is reluctant to give up homeruns, letting its counterpart in the right field become the source of Fenway's hitter's park reputation. Within the bleacher seats behind this squat, distance-challenged right field wall is the Lone Red Seat found in Section 42, Row 37, Seat 21 to be exact. It is the very landing spot Ted Williams hit the longest measurable homerun within the park. The smack occurred on June 9th, 1946, sending the ball the 502 feet into the stands, and hitting one allegedly napping Joseph A. Boucher directly atop his head.

The startled fan was later quoted to have said, "How far away must one sit to be safe in this park? I didn't even get the ball. They say it bounced a dozen rows higher, but after it hit my head, I was no longer interested. I couldn't see the ball. Nobody could. The sun was right in our eyes. All we could do was duck. I'm glad I did not stand up." (Wikipedia)

Fortunately our experience at Fenway went far better than that of Mr. Boucher. It was awesome being there, and I'm not even saying this as a baseball enthusiast, rather it was the way things played out. The decision to even go up to Fenway was a good one and suddenly taking

25

the chance on seeing the game made it spectacular. It was wandering out behind home plate and then finding seats with a couple of good Joe's to hang with. It was participating in some of Fenway's traditions such as singing along to Neil Diamond's "Sweet Caroline", and BAAH BAAH BAAAAH-ing right along with everybody else. Listen to the song, and then you'll know what I'm talking about. And, it was standing on our feet with everyone else there, cheering, and whooping it up when the final pitch was strike three and game going to the Sox. The walk out with some 32,000 fans high on the win was a mass of feel good, and a most perfect night cap. Our beautiful autumn night was filled with cheers, champs, and the joy of creating a superb memory.

MAKE WAY FOR DUCKLINGS

Sometimes, it's those unexpected little moments while on vacation that leave an indelible impression on one's mind. And so it was for this seek and find adventure we took part in. Our quest began with Kim's need to purchase a children's book featuring our current locale. Her reasoning, you can't go home empty handed to the niece and nephews. Yet inevitably, a book is found to be so adorable and pertinent to what we've been doing, she can't resist, and acquires one for our own library as well. Such was the case with the Boston treasure "Make Way for Ducklings."

Written by Robert McCloskey and published in 1941, generations of Bostonian children have been reading the adventures of a mother goose and her intrepid eight ducklings as they waddle past one hometown landmark after another. Simple pencil drawings depict the adorable fowlary with loving and timeless renderings. It's a fun and easy read, Kim and I knocked it out while waiting in the airport. And it's certainly one I'd recommend. Beloved by so many, honor and tribute was bestowed by the creation of wonderfully adorable statues of these quackers. It became Kim and my mission to visit the Boston's Public Gardens, and home to this friendly flock.

Our final morning in Boston was absolutely glorious. A brilliant blue sky back dropped the brightly shining sun. Its rays caressed and warmed autumnal breezes sweeping gently over the city streets. Not a more perfect day could there've been than this one, and no better an invitation extended to take a stroll in a park.

Enjoying the peacefulness of it all, Kim and I made our way to the Public Gardens and successfully hunted down those stationary ducks. Often we are easily entertained by the smallest of trivialities, but there before us was a ready-made adorable setting. Cast in iron and appearing as maternal as any duck can, led the proud mother goose. Close on her tail feathers were the dutiful ducklings in varied posed states. Interspersed among the inanimate creatures were busy toddlers and their doting parents hovering nearby. Some of the children saddled up and sat upon the cooperative waddlers, while others attempted to feed them grass, pebbles, or whatever came into hand. Photo opps obvious, parents and Kim alike snapped away.

Not to be out done, or inhibited by my advanced age over these little ones, I got right into the mix of things. Getting my hands on these friendly fouls, I felt each duck in appreciation of its artistry, and gratitude for those considerate enough to permit such a feeling. I mean that both in the emotional sense as well as the sensory one. Making my way down the line, I encountered one of the small chaps astride a duckling. Knowing I was being watched as I felt the head of the sat upon critter, I began talking to it. I then ran my hand along its neck and into the belly of the anticipating boy. Giving him a tickle, I said, "And here's another duckling." His giggle and his parents laughter, along with Kim and mine, all made for one of those moments in life looked back upon and remembered warmly with a smile.

The time to leave the park, and Boston itself, quickly drew near. Kim and I made our own way back onto the street and realized a third day of good luck and things going our way would be pushing it a bit, so the decision was made to take a taxi to the airport. All the trouble of getting here was behind us now, and we certainly didn't want to take the chance of running into it as we were leaving.

Unbeknownst to us, our cab ride would have us doing our last little bit of site seeing. Every big city has its own signature landmark, that when seen, is immediately associated with it. Boston's famed landmark would be one of its newest constructs, the Zakim/Bunker Hill Bridge. This bustling bridge is considered the widest cable-stayed bridge with its ten lanes open for traffic, one of which we happened to be occupying. I didn't know any of this as I sat in the backseat hoping the driver really was taking us to the airport, but it was kind of a neat note to end our trip on.

OUR BEST TO BOSTON

Everything about this trip was spontaneous and impulsive, and despite a couple of harried moments, was just a wonderful time. Kim and I only skimmed the surface of what Boston has to offer, and quite literally have started a list of places and things we want to do when we go back. And back we will go. It is amazing to me our American heritage, from its beginnings through today. I love any opportunity to explore, learn, and generally have a good time, and Boston provided all of this. So thanks go to Bean Town, all those BoSox lovin' fans, and especially to Kim for saying yes to my wild haired suggestion of going in the first place.

SITES UNSEEN TIPS

GETTING AROUND

Much is made of the ability to drive, getting about independently and such. However, all this autonomy is unnecessary when traveling to any big city, especially if it's an unfamiliar, congested, or construction filled place. I say, what city isn't one of those things. So the problems of taking a trip in a city as a person with limited vision becomes nearly the same as those impaired with sight. What is the best way to get around? I encourage everyone to check out some of these things before setting a single foot out of your home.

Public Transit: Pop onto the internet and check out your chosen destinations public transit system. Whether it's by bus, subway, or train, the route information are typically depicted and explained by that city's transit authority. Map out where you want to go, check if any of the public routes correspond, and decide if this is something you feel you can do with whatever ability you have. Also make sure you check out the fares, whether the transit system offers day or week long passes, and most importantly, if there are discounts for those who are differently abled. Depending on the city, often a rider must provide a pass or documentation of proof regarding an individual's impairment. Acquiring those things may be more hassle than it's worth, but that's for you to decide. A perk of blindness often comes with the use of guide dogs or canes for the blind, in that, these are tools readily recognized and accepted, therefore needing no further clarification.

Private Drivers: The most obvious of these would be taxi cabs, but also include limousine services. Again, do your homework to determine if this would be the best means to move about your chosen destination. Contacting these services by phone may lend to negotiating the price, but most services have pre-established fixed rates. Obviously this would be a more expensive form of transportation, and each individual will have to determine affordability for themselves.

Tour Buses: This is my personal preference when visiting any larger city. You can contact the visitor's bureau or go online to learn what that particular city has to offer. Obviously, the more tourist bound destinations will have greater options in touring. Put your "disability" to good use and inquire about discounts, pre-boarding, preferred seating. Take those perks if they are offered. I typically will utilize a city wide tour on the first day or two of travel to get the feel for the place, and to determine what points of interests I'll be seeing. I have also become very fond of the "hop on and off" tours that are becoming more prevalent. This type of touring allows for more freedom of choice in what you may want to visit. It's also helpful just in case you get one of the lame tour guides or are having difficulty hearing the PA system. That way you are not stuck once you're on.

MIND'S EYE

Who says you have to actually see it to have seen it? Not me, that's for sure. I'm a big believer of living the experience and letting my mind's eye enhance all I've done. Oh sure, I like to get my hands on stuff, matter of fact I'll be talking about that more later, but I don't let what I can't see take away from what I am doing. For instance, when I was talking about being in Boston's Bull and Finch bar, I let my mind's eye imagine that I really was in Cheers. Why not, it made the experience more fun for me. Did I need to see all 32,000 Red Sox fans to know the place was packed and having a great time? No way. Remember a perk of blindness is that you can always see things your way, you do not have to conform to all reality has to limit. You have the ability to make any site you are seeing that much better; so enjoy yourself and see the sites as I do, through my mind's eye.

2

NEW YORK, NEW YORK

Even if I used every digit on both my hands, plus those who live with me, including our dog and three cats, I still wouldn't have enough to represent how many times I've been to the big city of New York. As a child my family lived up in north Jersey, and it was there where my vision problems were first tended to. Trips into Mount Sinai hospital became a part of our family's regular routine, particularly when treatment began. My mother, grandfather, who I called Pop Pop, and I would travel in twice a week so I could get blood taken and then receive the wonderful Methotrexate injections that always had me throwing up on the ride home. Despite this youthful association to the city, I have since successfully repressed any further urges to vomit whenever I've visited New York. It's a good thing too, because I've been there at least three more times as an adult, and I'd like to share with you right now those adventures.

This first trip to New York involved a promise, a single minded teenager, and endless amounts of reminders. I speak of my lovely daughter Sarah holding me to the promise of taking her to see New York someday. The kid wore me down with her persistence, a trait she possesses in abundance. I'm sure I haven't the foggiest notion where she gets it from either. So a promise of someday became sooner rather than later, and was kept with a trip to New York City in what had to be the hottest, most humid summer ever on record, at least in my opinion. No matter, because Sarah, Kim and I wanted to see the Big Apple, and take in as much as we could of its offerings in a 48-hour period. Guidebooks and maps poured over, the sites picked out, we were ready for New York.

Home to millions and a dream to countless more, New York City's lure and lore transcends time and place. From young hopefuls wanting to make it big on the Great White Way, to immigrants seeking the chance of a better life, so many have crossed distances to be in this magical place. America's promise of liberty is made manifest by the Lady in the Harbor. Its grit and determination evidenced by the everyday people who continue on with their living, even when tragedy interrupts. New York has much to offer and experience, and regardless of the time of day, or night, the hum of the city is constant.

LIKE BUTTAH

I am the self-professed and well established travel nerd, who is easily excited by every adventure even if it's a repeat destination. For Sarah and Kim though, this was their first time to New York City and they were all a tingle with anticipation. It's no wonder nobody sat near us on the train trip into Penn Station from Jersey. We were blathering hyped up tourists, unable to help our own selves. Even if we could've we weren't really going to try, because taking pictures of each other and ooh-ing over the urban scenery was just too much fun, especially when the trapped train audience seemed somewhat entertained by our antics. Second thought, maybe they were grimacing. No matter. With nothing more than our backpacks, and opportunities lying in wait before us, we giddily rode into the great city of New York.

I knew it was gonna be, have even heard tales of it, but really being in the midst of it, living it, well, it's a whole other thing. I'm talking about how freakin' crowded New York City really is. Disembarking the train at Penn Station had us in first contact with the hordes of people that seemed to be absolutely everywhere. I'm thinking we could take a lesson or two from ants, who in their organized rank and file manage to find destination sought. We humans, have quite the opposite approach, darting, sauntering, waddling, stopping, are just some of the ways we were encumbered by the swarm all around us. It's as if the crowd itself becomes a living, breathing mass. And I guess figuratively speaking it would be true. But I mean it in quite another way.

A crowd could not "Be", without each individual present and contributing to the greater aspect of the entity. Every grouping we encountered had its own purpose and style of being. There was the initial train station crowd that was comprised of individuals moving towards their wanted destinations, as well as the street crowds that held a variety of peoples like the lookers, the movers, the workers and so on. Each has its own vibe to it. Maybe I've watched one to many Star Trek episodes, but I will testify for certain, the crowds of New York City have an essential pulse. Not to mention one other aspect; they're friggin big.

I've already shared this trip to New York was not my first, and it's very true in some sense, but in another, it's not. Let me explain. You already know of my childhood forays, but I've also ventured into the city in a more willing condition as a tourist, such as going on the eve of the eve of New Years. However, this was my first time to the city blind. So like my two darling novices, what I was about to do was all new and exciting. Under other circumstances, I may have been the person to take the literal lead as we moved about, but for obvious reasons I did not. Instead, I offered my travel expertise and great sense of direction.

Sarah's contribution to our city touring was most invaluable and truly amazing. That kid, she had the uncanny ability to cut through a crowded New York street like a hot knife through butter. Sidewalks cluttered with pedestrians and obstacles too numerous to mention—none mattered to Sarah. She weaved her way like a seasoned veteran of the street.

As if not impressive enough, let me strike you with awe at what I'm about to say next. Sarah's city agility never seemed hampered by that which she towed behind her—namely, me and Kim. My grasp firmly placed upon Sarah's weighted down shoulder, and Kim's upon mine, we congaed our way through throngs of people with nary a mishap. Oh, there was the occasional crack in the sidewalk, and "wreckoning" pothole attempting to twist my ankle, but this hardly slowed the mighty Sarah down. She was fine, it was just Kim and I who fumbled and bumbled along behind this newly teened steamroller.

CITY OVER VIEW

Okay, New York is a mighty big place. Our time there was very limited. So the means to get about it and see what we wanted needed to be efficient. More importantly, it had to be easy. Taxis being too expensive and subways not even on a dare, we decided upon a Double Decker Tour bus. The airy, roofless second level of the bus was a must seat for Sarah. Clambering up the narrow, twisted steps as the bus rolled presented some challenge, but was worth the vantage point with unhindered views of the city. It was also pretty cool to be eye level with the traffic lights and touch them, especially since we were told not to. Such naughty tourists we were.

Rolling along on the topless bus, the closest thing we had to air conditioning on this incredibly sticky hot, humid summer day was the exhaust fumes from the traffic surrounding us. The guide's words blasted over the PA system citing this factoid and that as we lumbered down the streets of New York. The first stand out site was once the tallest building in the world. The Empire State Building loomed large and high into the sky. I craned my neck as far as it would go without my head toppling off, to pretend look at it. I do this often when being shown places, giving the item a proper look for politeness sake; however, in doing such a thing as I did, it also permitted me perspective. My having to rearrange my vertebrae gave me an indication of just how high this building was. Furthermore, Kim has taken habit of drawing an outline with my finger of the structure, as well as the ones around it. In doing so, my view becomes clearer. And thanks to having seen when I could see, the movie King Kong, I had a basic remembrance as to the buildings actual appearance.

This incredibly famous building of the Empire State began its construction during the Great Depression, when the head honchos of Chrysler and GM raced to have the tallest building in the world. Obviously oblivious to the phallic symbolism, and the often subscribed sentiment of "size matters" metaphor, the GM fellow took tremendous pride in his victory. At 102 stories, the Empire State Building has shared starring roles in such famous movies as the already mentioned King Kong, as well as An Affair to Remember, When Harry Met Sally, and Sleepless in Seattle. A fact I found completely intriguing was the planned use of a mooring mast up atop the spire. If you recall, a means of transportation once used were dirigibles, or as we more commonly know them today, a blimp. The idea was for the dirigible to come floating along and anchor to this air dock. However wind gusts proved the task impossible, and the horrible unrelated fate of the Hindenburg concluded any further attempts.

We rolled on past this monolithic monument, knowing time would not be on our side this visit. Our bus cruised through Greenwich Village, the harbor area, pointed out Battery Park, the Brooklyn Bridge, and even showed us where Katharine Hepburn lived when she was alive. Central Park was a mere drive by and Times Square a jump off spot since we had our hotel there. We had gotten an overview of this portion of New York City, and soon, we'd be getting in touch with it.

TIMES SQUARE

From Ohio we had decided upon our accommodations, and were prepared for the upper echelon ilk of the Times Square Hilton. What we had no way of knowing was just how bad our collective appearance would be when arriving on its doorstep. Disheveled, over heated and rather ripe lumps of flesh might paint the picture accurately enough. I dare anyone to try running around New York in 90 plus degree weather, and then see how daisy fresh you'd be. It's somewhat amazing we were permitted in the door, much less up into the hotel lobby, but I guess the confirmation slip we had firmly in hand proved our right to be there. What could they do but let us in. Reservations baby, it's all about reservations. I'm sure the hotel had its own reservations, but we had the kind that got us in.

As it's been said before, location is everything; therefore the Hilton had it all. Right in the hub of this bubbling city, we walked easily anywhere we wanted. We hoofed up to the Hard Rock Cafe, down along 7th Street, to a tour bus stop, and most importantly, right across the street to Cold Stone Creamery. It was wonderfully convenient. But those high-faluting Hilton's didn't stop there, nope, 'cause they threw in great amenities like air conditioning, comfy beds, and a shower with free soap. Lordy be! Alright, so we could've gotten that at most any motel in the US. But the point is, this was New York City, and our less than high class selves were staying on Times Square.

We decided to do a little after houring, some site seeing by night, and with Times Square lying right at our feet, it's all good. They ain't kiddin' when saying New York is the city that never sleeps. The neon lights blazed from theater marquis and store front signs, displacing night with brilliant day-glow. We too glowed from all the iridescence, and felt less than alone, as we shared the experience with hundreds of others doing seemingly the same. The feel, vibe, pulse, whatever you want to call it, was catching and invigorating.

The Times Square area sprawls over many blocks and is home to the theater district, ABC headquarters, and the ultimate collection of billboards. So integral to the look of this spot, the city has passed into ordinance that all buildings not only display signs, but they must be covered in them as well. Tacky, possibly, but it's the shtick they went for. Once a place of ill repute, the Square cleaned up its act, got Disneyfied by the mouse with store and purchased theater, and has become a wholesome family locale. Times Square is also home to one of the most famous events known in the world, the New Year's Eve countdown. The first ball drop took place back in 1907, and has been falling annually ever since.

Typically New York is known for a variety of culinary delights, and yet we never once had a good meal there. Such was the case with a particular establishment called Roxy's Grill on Times Square. If you ever have the chance to eat there, DON'T! A little noshing needed, we ducked into this restaurant for a quick bite. C'mon, a deli in New York City, how can you miss? Somehow, we did. Service lacking, food mediocre at best, and prices being exorbitant, all made for a bad dining experience. I'll give it this though, the portions were huge. We ordered one turkey club sandwich that fed all three of us, but we had to be sneaky about sharing since a sign stated an extra charge would be tacked onto the bill if this was done. We got some Cole slaw and pickles that should've been ashamed to be identified as such, for they did not well represent their deli lineage by any stretch of the imagination. Covertly sharing a large, nothing to write home about piece of chocolate cake and drinking individual beverages, the sum of our meal came to a mere $42. That didn't include the nominal tip we left our mostly absent waiter. I'm telling you, next time we're going to McDonald's.

Our best touristy-type shopping occurred at 11 o'clock at night. I have taken to doing this sort of sordid thing on all my trips, giving into my touchy feely ways. I jones for it, until need is met. The seeking and feeling of the tourist trap souvenirs has completely been rationalized in my mind, and I'll now share the justification for trinkets with you all-purpose even.

No matter where you go to visit, there will inevitably be someone selling something there. You'll find a chintzy plastic snow globe, postcards, and of course, the obligatory T-shirts. These tchotchkes don't interest me, unless I'm shopping for someone else that is, but I don't want to digress. What I am looking for in all places I go is a small, preferably well-crafted representation of where I've been. This minute replica serves me in two ways. Holding it in my hand, I am seeing with my fingers what my eyes failed to give me out there in the world. It allows me clarity in picturing a place I have visited, and serves as a reminder when I take a look again at it when home. A friend coined the phrase of it being my 3D postcard. As those of you with sight might look at a photograph you have taken, I can grab hold and use both my fingers and mind's eye to recreate the visit.

I have provided you a purely justified tourist shopping rationale. It borders on noble I think. However, I feel the need to make a truthful declaration. I love souvenir shopping! Always have, even when I could see. The blind thing, it just gives it an honorable excuse to do it now. I didn't have to tell you this; you would've been none the wiser if I hadn't. I could also make the argument for this whole shopping compulsion being genetic, seeing that my father has the same problem, maybe another time. Know this though; my ability to see in the traditional sense may be diminished, but not my ability to rationalize.

Standing in the overly lit store at nearly midnight, I almost did a happy dance when I had in hand my 3D cityscape postcard. Sarah was just as thrilled when she found her collectable New York snow globe, not one of those cheap jobs either. It was also here Sarah came into contact with the legendary rudeness of New Yorkers.

The store was crowded and the lines long. We heard the cashier yell "Next!" This was the last word spoken semi-directly to us. None of the usual "Is there anything else," "Cash or credit," or "Have a nice day" was offered. The guy, who just happened to be foreign born and speaking the entire time in his native tongue to the worker next to him, obviously missed that day in customer courtesy class. Sarah, rather civil and well-mannered herself, got a bee in her bonnet over this one, and couldn't help but be annoyed by it all. I'm telling you, the way she kept bringing it up, I thought my grandmother had possibly possessed my kid.

Let me say this so as to not offend the truly good hearted citizens residing there in New York. We never once experienced this alleged rude way from anyone we met on the street, for in our ever seeking direction travels, all those we accosted were more than friendly and helpful. They were downright pleasant people to talk with. Like any other urban legend, misconceptions make for better stories, and in the process, New Yorkers have gotten a bum rap over the years. They're people too, just like in the Midwest, down south, anywhere you might go in these United States. I gotta say, give peace a chance and those kindly folks from the five boroughs too.

So would yous guys now take the hit off of me?

THE BROOKLYN BRIDGE

Although I have never been to the Brooklyn Bridge before, it manages to conjure up two memories in my mind. The first fond remembrance is that of the wascally wabbit himself, Bugs Bunny, while the second is, the TV show bearing the same moniker. I had spent many a wonderful hour as a child watching Bugs' antics, clearly recalling how he drove poor ole Jim Brody Looney tunes and right off the Brooklyn Bridge. And I loved that exceptional, albeit short-lived, CBS show with Marion Ross as the Yiddish speaking Jewish grandmother. Both are fond recollections of television from my younger days, resulting in a warm fuzzy feeling towards this big old inanimate object itself. So when a trip to the Big Apple was decided upon, I knew that my site must see had to be the Brooklyn Bridge.

Since 1883, the Brooklyn Bridge has spanned New York's East River, beginning what could be called the ultimate urban sprawl. Connecting Manhattan to rural Brooklyn enabled New York City's limits to envelop and develop this area into what it is today. Millions have traveled over this iconic suspension bridge, and now it was our turn.

Excitedly I hopped off the tour bus and urged my companions forward to the entry way. As I followed Sarah, trusted guiding quickly became questioned, for it seemed as though we were headed directly into the racing traffic coming over the bridge. To say I was feeling a little freaked out as cars, trucks, and other means of death whizzed by, would be a gross understatement. Despite assurances we were securely on a sidewalk and protected by some fencing, my natural instinct to fear large, rapidly moving vehicles inches from me could not be silenced. I'm sure it was safe, but I couldn't help the once gentle grasp placed upon Sarah's shoulder becoming a fear induced vice grip.

Venturing further out onto the bridge became a little more calming with not being directly next to the traffic. I was able to focus my attention better and took time to feel some of the pieces and parts of this historic bridge. Kim was thrilled with having two of her favorite things right before her, photo opps, and countless plaques and signs waiting to be read. The bridge offered its own history lesson, sharing facts and figures of size and length, strands of cable used, and other such technical aspects of the bridge's making.

The more personal tidbits included the visionary planner John Robling. He was driven by the inspiration of connecting the lands, and to be honest, make some money in the process. Nobody ever said visionaries can't use financial gain to inspire them. Thousands of men worked on the bridge's construction in very dangerous conditions. From the height of the towers, to the depths of the anchors keeping the Brooklyn Bridge in place, these men risked life and limb in its construction.

The marvel of this great American construct was worth making the pilgrimage. I initially wanted to be there because of stories built around the bridges presence, but it's the reality of the people who saw the need, and worked till the Brooklyn Bridge's completion, that are truly the stories to honor.

STREET FIGHT

There are moments when everything seems to slow. Peace falls like a gentle rain, and a calming bliss soothes one's soul. I'm gonna tell you right now, this wasn't one of them.

Tranquility is especially impossible when a body is over-heated, over hungry, and really confused. Triple those things, and you'd have the perfect description of our worn out, frazzled selves. These kinds of situations can only lead in one of two directions, tears or anger. And, let me tell you, nobody felt like crying.

Our collective meltdown took place on the corner of I Dunno and What the F*   *   *. Adults and child alike stood toe to toe blasting unheard words at one another. The provocation setting the tinder into full flame was the same old thing we fight about on every trip. We needed direction and a decision. Anger abounded, as did Kim's gesturing hands and arms as they flailed wildly. I can only speak to my state of mind, which was none too pretty at the time. I was well past losing it, and teetered on being quite deranged.

Apparently the universe was feeling impish that day, because some street musician dude decided just then to pick up his horn and blow. I swear it couldn't have been more than a foot from my face. He had absolutely no idea of the peril he was in, with coming this close to swallowing the thing. Moving from the corner became imperative with my not wanting to be jailed for assault, although the victims of choice were a toss-up at the time. My last nerve was down to its final fray between Kim's insistent need to explain herself, and the horn blowing fool. Unled, I walked away. Sarah understood to silently follow. And Kim, she was back there still talking while the man played on.

Direction was determined with my sudden movement, and decision followed as I told Sarah to go directly into the first place serving food. Who cares that it was some skanky hole in the wall pizza place. It gave us exactly what we needed, food fast, a chance to regroup, and a place to cool down in more than one way. Love was restored, along with our ability to think more clearly. I guess I was wrong with my original assumption then. Peace and calm is possible for us in New York, at least with the purchase of pizza.

LADY LIBERTY'S ISLAND

Without question, the ultimate birthday gift has got to be the Statue of Liberty. In honor of the United States' centennial, France saw fit to create such an impressive tribute to liberty, democracy, and freedom. And nobody quibbled about it being delivered ten years late either, because in 1886, the American people celebrated as the beautiful Lady of Liberty found her new home in New York City's harbor.

There are a few very interesting "I didn't knows" I came across, and thought fascinating enough to share about Ms. Liberty. First, as I already mentioned, the statue was to be a centennial gift to the United States. France's friendship began during the Revolutionary War when it became our allies. The gift celebrated both this long time friendship between nations, as well as America's birth. So the sculptor Frederic Auguste Bartholdi intentionally inscribed into the book in her hand, "JULY IV MDCCLXXVI". Translated, this would be July 4, 1776.

Artists love symbolism, and our lady's crown with the seven rays is no exception. Each ray represents the seven continents of the world signifying her purpose is expansive and inclusive of all. I didn't know before this trip of the broken shackles lying at her feet, which are representative of tyranny and oppression. These are obviously relevant to the impetus of the colonies fight for freedom and the founding of our country. Yet I find her meaning to be even more impressive when taken in historical context of the time she arrived. For the United States was only twenty years out from its own Civil War, and all this lady stood for, was very relevant to what the country faced.

I could go on about her green pallor being the weathered copper she is made of, or cite her measurements and weight, but I wouldn't want to be rude to such a fine lady, Instead, I think I'll turn my attention to our little jaunt over for a visit. Not unlike the Wicked Witch of the West whose life changed greatly with a little water tossed her way, we too experienced the melting effect as a result of intense humidity. Throw in some heat, and what do you get, Sarah Soup. The poor kid only wanted to see the Statue of Liberty up close; she didn't ask to be a people puddle. Full enjoyment potential was impossible, but she surely did try.

Making our way through Battery Park in search of the ferry to Liberty Island, we first found some really creepy looking people dressed in the statue's garb and painted green. These mime-esque individuals apparently were to draw the crowds in, but if it weren't for the real deal standing in wait just beyond them, I think Sarah would have high-tailed it right out of there. The security screening was organized and efficient, as was the boarding of the ferry, so in no time we arrived and set foot on Liberty Island.

Unsure as to my island orientation, and wanting to know where I was, I asked frequently for a clue. Kim tried to give me a more technical answer, using angles, degrees, and possibly a few geometry terms I've long since forgotten, much less ever really learned. Sarah however, not in the mood for my stupidity, cut right to it and said, "We're by her armpit." Bingo! I knew exactly our whereabouts at that very moment and pictured my being next to the statue. Further using the finger painting trick to get perspective, Kim traced the lady's outline, enabling me to complete the picture in my mind.

As one does when in front of any historic monument, we took turns posing and snapping each other's pictures. This also is when accosting strangers is acceptable, is practically a tourist requirement, all in the hopes of capturing the perfect group photo. And let me just give a little plug for digital cameras. In the old days of film photography, you had to just hope and pray the person who took your picture knew what they were doing. How many times have the traveled gotten home, developed their film with excited anticipation, only to find body parts missing, pictures blurred, or a memento of that stranger's thumb. No more though with today's digital cameras. Now we can have the instant look, give direction for a re-take, or attempt to find a more apt individual to snap into immortality the moment of a lifetime.

The heat and blazing sun became too much for Sarah, and she made it known by turning into a gooey mass right in front of us. Kim, seemingly unaffected and hyped up by the up close and personal encounter with the Lady, kept on taking pics, as Sarah and I retreated to a nice shady spot. Sipping a little water, lying in the cool grass under a nice shade tree, and relaxing did wonders for my girl.

Unfortunately, I think appreciation for the Statue of Liberty may have been more in the anticipation phase of this trip. Next time though, we'll do our visiting in a much cooler month than July, and have more time to devote to some of the inside attractions. None the less, we wouldn't have missed it for the world.

ELLIS ISLAND

Without a doubt, Ellis Island was the most anticipated part of the trip for each of us. Pulling together the historical significance and our own personal family connection, Ellis Island didn't fail my expectations one little bit. I had hoped to be making this New York trip with my mother, but an unseemly accident involving a soccer ball and the resulting busted hip, clearly put any notions of a multi-generational visit out of reach.

From its opening day in 1892 through its closing in 1954, Ellis Island was the gateway into America for more than twelve million immigrants. But it was only three of those millions who inspired us to be present on this particular day. And although the temperature was closing in on a hundred degrees, I tried to imagine what it might have been like on a very different kind of day.

It was one of those bitterly cold days in March where shades of gray barely distinguish sea from sky. Out on the horizon, yet another ship seeks port as it carries hopeful passengers. A small girl shivers as she stands at the ice covered rail, peering expectantly into the distance. Not believing her own eyes, she glimpses through the wintry mist the sight of a woman standing on the water. Eyes transfixed, the girl watches as this lady rises tall and reveals herself. It is the welcome so many had seen before her, it was, the Statue of Liberty. And the girl knew her new home was near.

Being merely ten years old, the girl remembered little else of her arrival. She depended on her parents to keep her safe in the vast crowd of people. She followed closely, holding her mother's hand as all of them moved into a cavernous, darkened building. The girl didn't know what was happening, was too overwhelmed to remember the details. She only knew it was loud and crowded.

That little ten year old girl was my mother, Doris Kaiser. In 1952, just two years before Ellis Island processed its last batch of immigrants, my mother and my grandparents, Karl and Erika Kaiser, emigrated from Germany to the United States. Their story probably was very similar to so many others, but I find it uniquely interesting, seeing that it speaks directly to my family. Our visit to Ellis Island was more about paying honor to the accomplishments of many, and particularly, to my grandparents and mother. Although I'll tell you right now, my mother would say, and has said, she was just a kid who didn't know nothing and did what her parents told her to do. That doesn't make her story any less amazing if you ask me.

The Ellis Island tour is part of the Statue of Liberty circuit, which means we got on and off the same ferry boat to arrive there. Entering the building, we were greeted by a man dressed in period clothing of typical immigrants from the late 1800's to the early 1900's. We learned from him of a short play on the immigrant experience and all agreed it would be a worthwhile investment to take it in. I was suspect at first when I heard a rather lame version of a present day Jamaican accent, but by play's end I was completely invested, and nearly moved to tears. All those people, what they went through to come to America, the chances they took, the hope they had, was amazing. I couldn't help but project what my own mother and grandparents may have undergone in their own immigration process to America.

Ellis Island is now a museum of wonderful artifacts related to the immigrant experience. From clothing to luggage, many items are on display, along with countless pictures and gobs of information for the reading. Additionally, a wonderful information desk is present to help individuals trace their ancestor's arrivals. Time is needed in going through such incredible historical items, and this was something we were all too quickly running out of.

We went in search of our own piece of history, and found the KARL J. KAISER FAMILY plaque on the Wall of Honor. I felt the engraved name and despite knowing it, I still was amazed this was my family. The wall itself stretched on, two-sided, with thousands of individual and family names upon it. One tiny inscription represented my remarkable grandparents, Karl and Erika, the hope they had, the drive to see it through, and the wonderful life they made for themselves, their children, and the rest of us. It also represents my mother's entrance into this country, and the unknown. She had to do a lot of trusting and learning, which has led to her becoming a woman I love and respect like no other.

I was bursting with pride. My emotion culminated and drove me to action. I called my mother! I desperately wanted to share this with her and the only way was by phone. So Sarah and I chatted with Mom and vowed, we're coming back to Ellis Island, No ifs, ands, or buts about it, Doris Kaiser Walker will be there with us.

PLACED IN OUR PATH

Who among us doesn't still experience a moment's hesitation when thinking of September 11th? Our trip to New York was a mere four years after this horrific event and the wound in the city landscape still lay open. The tons of debris had been cleared away, but the expansive crater remained, not yet ready for reconstruction. As the ground lay unready, so too was I with the idea of visiting ground zero. It was Kim and Sarah who wanted to be there, and see for themselves this hallowed place.

We walked from Battery Park to the former site of the World Trade Towers, emerging from some side street, and suddenly came upon the vast hole left behind. Kim outlined the circumference with my finger, and I was struck by the sheer size of the vacancy. We stood silently holding onto the safety fencing erected around this area. The sounds of the city seemed to dissipate, leaving the lone wail of the subway cars passing below on its resurrected rail.

I was surprised with my reaction of being here. I did not feel sadness, anger, or any of the emotions I had expected. Instead, it all provoked a quiet remembrance and thoughts of hope. Hundreds of lives were lost that day, and countless more have been altered forever. I cannot begin to imagine how those directly touched by the events on that beautiful September morning have coped and persisted on with their lives. I can only believe something good can come from this. Call it hope, faith, karma, whatever you will, just believe it.

I wasn't looking for a spiritual experience while there. To be honest, I only wanted to get it over with. But sometimes it's the things that find you when you're not even looking, that can be the most profound. And Kim was about to learn this. I guess we all were.

The walk back from Ground Zero provided the typical city obstacles of uneven curbs, street vendors, and of course, construction. Add to that the heat of the day, fatigue from all already accomplished, and a sense of urgency to return to the bus, it's amazing anything could be noticed. Among sidewalk cracks and loose gravel, something glistened, catching Kim's eye. A small silver cross had broken away from its wearer and lay on the ground, as if waiting there. Kim will tell you how she passed it by, but her attempt to ignore this small symbol of hope and faith would not allow it. The need to retrace her steps and claim the cross was too great.

I cannot speak for Kim as to the meaning she takes from this, it's not my place. Instead I prefer to share my own thoughts. Both literally and figuratively along life's pathways there are opportunities lying in wait. Some might be more obvious than others. I guess it then becomes our decision, whether to grab it up, or ignore it. The same truth applies to the people who may share a bit of that life path with you. Yours may unexpectedly cross with an individual who might just be a symbol of hope and faith. One never knows when this might occur, and certainly wouldn't think a bathroom need would be the catalyst leading to the opportunity.

Our two-day romp and stomp in the big city had come to an end. Catching the train back to Jersey was the last bit of traveling needing to be done. Sarah, Kim and I felt the fatigue of our whirlwind excursion yet were still spry enough to hold a recapping discussion, at least until Sarah had other pressing matters made known. Not knowing the train had what Sarah needed and saying as much, a fellow passenger kindly spoke up and directed much to Sarah's relief. The ice was broken with small talk, giving way to a most moving revelation, and uplifting conversation.

Typical stranger-polite-speak where basic information is easily exchanged, inevitably gets around to what line of work people are in. This conversation was no different. Yet in learning of her work, we soon found out our stranger witnessed the events of September 11th first hand. Her office view was directly upon the World Trade Towers, and she watched as the first tower burned. In stunned disbelief she witnessed the plane as it crashed into the second Trade Center building, and realized the unbelievable was happening. She spoke of the building evacuation, the crowded streets, and the miles walked as everyone sought refuge outside the city. We listened with rapt attention as she shared her story and were drawn in even further as she spoke of her personal beliefs. In the days and months following, she witnessed the goodness of others, people at their best when the worst had taken place. Her faith in God and mankind was lifted, as it never had been before.

Four people were drawn to the same place and time. By being open to the opportunity before us, we connected and affected one another. This is truly a beautiful gift. Our encounter reaffirmed what I believe on many levels, and for Kim, I think it was a needed reminder. Sarah remained silent, absorbing what she heard. I could feel her heart grow as she leaned across my lap to listen more closely. Our souls were opened and enriched by the miracle of an everyday person speaking of an extraordinary experience. And this woman who was heading home from another day of work, I can only hope she took with her continued healing and faith. Four people, four paths, and one incredible chance meeting.

NEW YORK REVISITED

Since the quick trip to New York City with Kim and Sarah, I've been back to the Big Apple a couple more times; each even shorter than the first. I sure don't know why I've got to get in and out of New York so quickly, it's not an aversion to being there or anything intentional, it's just how things end up.

The first trip back was in response to my friend Vicki asking me to accompany her. She had been invited to an award ceremony, in which she was one of the winners. This whole story involves some explaining, and me rewinding just a bit. It all started when Vicki took me to China. Yes, I said "took me" and yes, to the other side of the world. Vic travels a tremendous amount for her work. With all this flying about, she racks up the frequent flyer miles and on the occasion, she extends her incredibly generous self. Actually, she always has her heart open like this, but sometimes the generosity is unbelievably grand.

One day, whenever ago, Vicki learned a bit about me in our church newsletter. In it I had stated my love of travel and some of the places I'd already been. Making small talk, she shared her own globe-trotting affinity and casually said something like, "You should come along with me to China." Mind you, the words are not exact but the gist was gotten, and I tucked the invite somewhere safely in my brain. To be more truthful, I ruminated a while, kind of occasionally felt Vicki out to see if she was just being polite, and months later, commenced to reminding her of her offer. What can I say; I'm a brazen blind broad who won't ignore opportunity's knocking. We did go to China for an incredible eleven days, a story I hope to tell another time, but I best be getting to the one I already started.

Several months later Vicki received a contest offer asking its frequent flyers to submit a 100 word story about their best trip ever. Vic wrote a blurb about our China trip, seeing it in a whole new way like through my eyes sort of thing. Kitschy, I agree, but she won the big prize with it, a roundtrip for two to Australia. It seems the sighted can benefit too from the perks of blindness. I'm gonna digress for half a sec here and tell you, even though I was Vicki's inspiration that won her that big free trip, you know, the wind beneath her wings, she didn't see things my way when I pled my case to be her travel buddy once again to the land down under. Can you believe she took her spouse instead? Go figure.

In lieu of the trip of a lifetime, I got the consolation prize. Vicki invited me to accompany her to New York City to attend the awards banquet. Being a grateful beggar, I took her up on it and had loads of fun as we hit the city hard and fast. Our plane touched down at LaGuardia Airport the evening before the big to-do, requiring we entertain our own selves until its start. Cabbed and hoteled, we sought out and found our first impromptu venture.

Most folks wouldn't dare think about walking the streets of New York after dark. It would give one pause to do so. The fact it was now winter, late January even, the sound of mind would likely shudder at the thought—yet there Vic and I were, cruising the street on foot. If balmy and January can be used in the same sentence when describing New York weather, I'll use it now. For as certain as it was the first month of the year, it was at least in the non-frost bite temperature range as we strode along in search of a bite to eat.

On our culinary radar was the one and only home of the seven ounce burgers, the Jackson Hole diner. There's nothing better than sinking your teeth into a burger, unless there's a bigger one to be had. At Jackson Hole there is. Imagine a juicy heap of ground meat piled high with condiments and decorative vegetation, surrounded by an all-encompassing bun. My God, its heaven on earth I tell you. By the way, their veggie offering is some of the best french fries going. Vic and I partook in the diner's deliciosities, although my memory is foggy about what she had. I was totally consumed with my own platter and its consumption.

Stuffed silly and needing a good burping, Vic opted to walk me instead. I agreed as long as we didn't move too fast, and we didn't as we inched our way over to the gas station quickie-mart next to our hotel. Something the state of New York has that Ohio doesn't, at least at the time of our trip, was one of those multi state lotteries. You know what I mean, where the pots get up into the bazillion dollar range. Vic bought a couple of those lottery tickets, a good idea since she was already on a winning streak. As far as I know though, the only thing she won that night was the pleasure of my company.

I was awakened the following morning by the uncustomary sounds of whizzing traffic and horns honking. Vic, who I believe rarely sleeps, was already up and tending to her blackberry. She's one of those mover and shaker types; don'cha know. The part of the trip that I was dreading the most was now upon me, getting dressed up. You see, when I eagerly agreed to attend this gig, I hadn't really thought the thing through. I'm a casual kind of gal. I basically have three pairs of shoes, and two of them are sneakers. I've got my good going out jeans, and the other pair for bumming around in. I wear T-shirts either under sweatshirts or button downs. I dress for comfort, that's who I am. This banquet was anything but me. I sucked it up though and pulled good clothes from the inner recesses of my home closet. You know the outfit I'm talking about, the kind worn inter-changeably to weddings and funerals. I rooted around until I finally found my old black shoes and was given permission by Kim to wear the entire attire in New York.

We had several hours to kill before the big award banquet was to begin. Just my luck, I was finally all dressed up and had no place to go. We did have to get out of the hotel room, and didn't want to be draggin' our bags around, so the decision was summarily made to find the banquet place, ditch our stuff, and find something with which to entertain ourselves for a while.

Central Park just happened to be directly across the street from our destination, and since we were both looking so good, Vic and I thought we should do a little something special. A ride through Central Park by Hansom cab was in order. Ever so conveniently a stand was located nearby, and even more convenient was the availability. Clambering atop the horse drawn buggy, we borrowed the available blanket and hunkered down to keep warm. A fleeting thought was given to smelling of equine at the reception, but quickly forgotten with the chill of winter's wind blowing.

Most likely this ride would have been far more enjoyable in another season, nonetheless, simple pleasures became evident. I loved the sound of the horse's footfall on paved road. The clip-clop of the hooves provided a kind of peaceful tempo as we rolled through the park. Our cabby was a sweet Irish man; his brogue was as delightful as his personality. He pointed out playgrounds, the direction of the Central Park zoo, and informed there was really no Central Perk coffee house as seen on the TV show Friends. Despite the quaintness of a buggy ride and the efforts of the thick horse blanket trying to keep us warm, Vic and I agreed this was a tad insane to be doing in the middle of winter—at least in our dressed up under dressed state anyway. Touristy antics over with, it was time for decorum and hob knobbing among the elite. If ever there's a place where you don't exactly fit in, don't know what is going to happen, and don't know nobody, Vicki is the woman you want by your side. Adept in the art of schmooze, and genuinely a friendly person, she can put anyone from ill to ease in no time. I initially felt out of sorts, but decided what the hell; these people will never see me again, an occasional dangerous philosophy to have. Although it served me well, for I loosened up and just had fun.

The entire purpose of this big New York banquet was to celebrate the best in the travel industry according to Traveler's magazine. There were folks from all over the globe, like the Korean flight attendants sitting at our table, not speaking a lick of English. These high fliers were chosen as best in this category because they entertain their customers during the flight by doing magic tricks. Who knew pulling a coin out of someone's ear could win them the big prize. I'm sure their super model gorgeous appearance didn't hurt their chances either. I kept imagining a flight with them would be like Baywatch at 30,000 feet.

All the travel industry winners were present to accept their awards and get photos snapped for the next issue of the magazine. Vic and I were there for a way better reason though, we were gonna meet a celebrity.

The person handing out the awards was Cynthia Nixon of Sex in the City fame. Alright, I'll be honest. Vicki was there for her, as a fan of the show. Me, I'd never seen an episode, but I knew I'd get some free stuff, and the chance to hang with Vic always sets me in motion. We encountered Ms. Nixon twice, the first prior to the sit down portion of the extravaganza. Some dude representing the airlines providing the free Aussie trip parted the crowds and took us over to meet the celeb. I'll have to say I was rather impressed with Ms. Nixon's warmth when we were introduced to her. She appeared to be genuine in her interest of who we were and graciously listened during our brief encounter. I'll not permit myself any cynical thinking to slip in here and remind myself she's an accomplished actress who was probably being paid a lot of dough to be there. Instead, I'll assume the best and give an example to prove it momentarily.

A lot of folks were waiting for their fifteen seconds of fame brushing, so quicker than we arrived, we were swept away. It's really intriguing to me how this phenomenon occurs. One second a body, like me, is engaged, and the next, I'm at the back of the room again. It's not unlike what a sea shell in the ocean experiences I'm guessing. One day it's sitting at the bottom of the ocean, minding its own business. Next thing it knows, it's riding a current and finds itself up on the beach. Assuming a shell has the capability of thought, it would think, "Hey, look at me!" And before it knows what hit it, a wave surrounds our little shell and sweeps it right back where it started. Both the ocean and the celeb machine get the job done, and me and the shell just go along for the ride.

Our second meeting was way cooler though. Sitting at our tables in the jammed pack reception hall, Vic and I perused our freebies, chowed down, and listened to the varied winners of this and that category be announced. Vicki, now adept at description from our eleven day excursion of the Far East, provided a picture perfect play by play of the goings-on. Then the big moment arrived, the introduction of this year's Traveler Magazine well-traveled person. Okay, that wasn't exactly the title crowned, but its close enough.

Vicki had prepared me by describing the lay of the land. How the room was set up, where the stage was, and so on. I could tell all by myself how crowded the place was between the sounds of talk and applause, not to mention the original negotiating the room when entering. But to be quite honest, it gets forgotten when you have to get up in front of all those on lookers. I can't speak for other blind folks, but when I'm really tired, or in this case, not wanting to make a fool of myself, my brain's connection to my stick is gone. My stick becomes this big pole thingy in my hand telling me absolutely nothing. However, to those around me, it becomes something altogether different. My blind stick becomes the staff of Moses and wields the same power he used to part the Red Sea. As Vicki loves to recount, she and I got up from our table and made the move towards the stage. The confined aisle way opened up wide as those sitting in their chairs realized we needed through. People jumped from their seats and all but catapulted out of the way. Any perceived obstacle was quickly removed from our path, and as we approached the steps leading up to the stage, I could feel the crowd holding their collective breath.

The good thing about tandem travel is I'm not all alone in what I'm doing. The really great thing about Vicki as a guide is she is completely trustworthy. And for that split second at the bottom of the steps when all eyes were on us, I thought 'this would really suck if I tripped.' It would make for better story telling if something dramatic happened at this moment, but all I did was walk up the two steps—sorry to disappoint.

Once on stage, Vicki received her award from Cynthia Nixon and some guys in suits. The obligatory picture taking was next, and this is where I found out Ms. Nixon is a swell gal. When a person has perfectly good vision they naturally fall into position and face the camera. When eyesight is a little gone, this ability to sidle up to those next to you properly is just not there. I mean really, my only means of figuring logistics out would be to feel about either with stick or hands. To be quite honest, it's probably not kosher to be copping a feel of strangers even if it's justifiably necessary. And another thing, those directions so often given of "straight ahead" are completely absurd. Straight ahead is relative and depends upon which way you're facing to begin with. If I'm facing one way and cast my gaze forward that my friend is straight ahead for me, no matter where you are. Don't get me started either with folks being clueless about clock directions in this age of digital.

Where'd my point go? Oh yeah, Cynthia being swell.

There we were, about five or six of us falling into formation for the pictures. I was doing my level best, turning kind of back in the direction we had come from. I had lost contact with Vicki since she had to step forward to grab her trophy. Standing there and hoping for the best, I assumed the photo pose and smiled. All of a sudden I felt gentle hands on both my shoulders from behind. Somehow, in my stage wanderings, I had gotten the spot right next to Cynthia. She softly steered me in the right direction while saying, "Just a little bit this way." Such a simple act of kindness. She didn't have to do it, wasn't responsible for me or the photo, but she did it anyway. It's those kinds of little things I believe are truly genuine and demonstrates the goodness of others. I have to say, it's good to know that Cynthia Nixon had my back that day.

As for the rest of the trip, it was pretty uneventful. Vicki and I did do some street walking but not for long since we had to catch our plane out of LaGuardia. By the way, what a dump that place is. The antithesis of today's modern airports would be this one. Yet it got the job done with a cheap flight and being on time. Our twenty-eight hour romp to New York was over with, and I have to say, hanging with Vicki is absolutely some of the best times I've had in my life. I jokingly say I continue to give her opportunities to show how great a person she is, with being generous and all. Thing is, with or without all this travel hoopla, she really is a wonderful woman, and I'm grateful for her friendship. Oh, and just to let you know, Vic's flying to Mexico a lot for work these days. Hmmm, south of the border sounds good to me.

BEFORE IT'S GONE

What do the Bronx, baseball, and the Pope all have in common? If your guessing it's the set up for a joke, you'd be wrong. If your answer indicated a type of cheer, or something to cheer about, you'd be technically correct. However, I was actually going for the segueing answer of Yankee Stadium. This iconic field of dreams is located in the heart of the Bronx and has held countless cheering fans of the game since 1923. More than home to the winningest team in baseball, the New York Yankees, the stadium has hosted events from football games, to concerts, boxing matches, and a couple of Pope's to boot.

Kim and I had an already planned vacation with my family in the summer of 2008, but when we realized this was the last season the historic Yankee Stadium would be around, we knew a side trip was in order. Oh sure, the Bronx is definitely a hop, skip, and a side trip from the Jersey shore. Nonetheless, we deemed it do-able once we learned the Yanks were going to be in town and we tracked down tickets on the web. Actually, that was the easy part. It was the drive to and in the Bronx that had us doubting. Although Kim has been driving for years without incident, and she is a pointless driver, meaning she has no ticket points on her license, she is not necessarily a confident big city driver. At least she isn't when it's a foreign city with a reputation of not being the safest to be wandering about. That's what we hear in Ohio anyway.

We stewed for a while about what to do. I obviously was of no use co-piloting, and reading maps while maneuvering speedy highways and city traffic just didn't sound like a good idea. It was time to invest in a relationship, and quite possibly a life saver, so we purchased a GPS navigational device, and promptly named her Maggie. I am of the mindset, and have been for years with my JAWS speech program on my computer, that anything talking to me that much must have a name. Hotel reserved as close to the stadium as possible, tickets stowed in pockets, directions, entered, off we went in my Mom's car to the Bronx.

A mere five hours later and a few laps around the stadium, I'll say for sight-seeing reasons, we arrived at our hotel—well, almost. Maggie will announce "You have arrived" when destination is actually met. Kim saw the sign for the hotel, a parking lot, and naturally assumed Maggie was sleeping on the job. Parking into said lot, I began emptying our trunk as Kim tucked items away not wanting to tempt any bad guys. Suddenly someone was standing next to me and said, "Who are you?"

I was taken aback but confronted this person by replying, "Who are, you?" Wanting to present a toughness so as to not be victimized my first thirty seconds in the Bronx, I stood as tall as my five foot almost ten frame allowed, and placed my stick in front of me more in a defensive posture than useful one. There was a slight pause before his response, and I heard, "I'm Officer blahdy blahdy blah." Okay, I'm sure he inserted his name there, but I was still stuck back on the cop portion of the conversation. I quickly learned that Kim had pulled into the local police department lot and had parked in one of the captain's spots. Oops, or something like that is what I'm sure I thought. Kim had finally emerged from the car, and once mistake was realized, she sought direction. I think Officer Blahdy was only too happy to get rid of us, so he obliged and directed us the additional fifty feet we had to go to be in the correct parking lot.

We had pre-decided to get a hotel near the stadium so as to walk there by day, and cab it home at night. However nerves already frazzled, we altered plans at check in and arranged a ride over to the stadium. I'm thinking it was only a few blocks, but sometimes easing effort is more precious than money.

I think maybe I should do a little bit of explaining as to why Kim and I risked life and my mother's car just to catch a baseball game. Being a Cleveland Indians fan, this wasn't so much about the Yankees of today; rather, it was completely about being a part of something bigger. To actively participate in the incredible history of Yankees Stadium by catching a game, seemed an opportunity that shouldn't be squandered. Knowing the plans for demolition following the 2008 season was one thing when in our Cleveland area home, but when we realized we would be so close; Kim and I knew we had to partake in this historic phenomenon.

Dropped at the entrance gate of Monument Park, a section of Yankees Stadium I will explain further in a moment, Kim and I soon learned that even though we were already to get in, the stadium folks weren't. We had another hour to kill before entering, so we kind of just stood around. Clump by clump the folks trickled in to form a crowd, and it was only then we learned two more important pieces of information.

First, we were in the wrong spot to actually gain entry into Monument Park. It was kind of the close but no cigar scenario, in that; Kim could see where we were supposed to be, but we weren't technically in line. All our waiting went for naught. Despite being the first people there, we were now dashing for the end of a really long line. To make matters worse, the second lesson took place as we slowly inched closer to the entrance.

The couple months before when Kim and I purchased our tickets via a broker, a.k.a. legal ticket scalper, we decided to get the economy seats. Hell, we were wanting in so we could wander, check out the way upper decks, circulate around a bit. I could've sat anywhere listening to the game and said I was at Yankee Stadium, and for some people that's enough, but not for me. I wanted to get my hands on the place and see it my way. All the description in the world isn't going to be the same as the actual hands on experience.

Since we didn't really intend on sitting in our seats all that much, we bought the cheapest available. This means, as it always does in any ball park, the bleachers. What we didn't know until standing at the gate, was this crazy ticket policy Yankee Stadium has. Get this, those holding bleacher tickets are designated to enter the stadium through a specifically assigned single gate. It gets worse though, because it is here where segregation occurs. A sort of classism. The cheap seats might get you in the back door, but not into the stadium itself. I never heard of anything so ridiculous, and discriminatory.

We couldn't believe our ears. Our minds unwilling to accept such a bizarre rule as real, we decided to seek clarification. Approaching a stadium employee, we asked and received confirmation in one fell swoop. I'll be honest, I don't know what ran through Kim's mind at this moment, but I can tell you I was stunned. I think the clichéd dropped jaw would aptly describe my shocked appearance. I felt the excitement of our being at Yankee Stadium slip away and be replaced by rejection. I didn't argue, I just kind of babbled about not being told this when we bought our tickets. I shared how we came all the way from Ohio just to have the chance to be in Yankee Stadium. Ever so politely, Mr.

Stadium Guy apologized as we dejectedly turned on our heels and walked away.

Disappointment seeped into every fiber of our being and reshaped us into what could only be described as pitiful lumps of flesh. Heads no longer held high with anticipation, and shoulders hunched as the air of excitement leaked out, we moved away from the promise land to find our second class seating. Then I heard it, a single word of hope. "Wait." As quick as we felt our dreams kicked to the curb, optimism returned. About facing, we were before the man once more, puppy doggedly looking up at him. He then said, "If you promise to just go in and come right back out, I'll let you in." Throwing up my hand in oath-like manner, I swore my agreement. It was that, or leap over the rail separating us and giving him a big kiss. This wonderful, albeit rule breaking man allowed us entrance into a once in a lifetime opportunity.

MONUMENT PARK

Famed Yankees Lou Gehrig, Babe Ruth, and manager Miller Huggins, were all honored back in the day with monuments dedicated to their contributions to baseball. Originally they were placed in fair territory of the playing field, and on the occasion, a ball would be hit there. Those are the simple facts of the game. And now here are some of the colorful legends that make baseball so great. One day, a hit got by a Yankees outfielder and ended up amongst the monuments. The ball player scrambled and had trouble coming up with it. The great Yankee manager Casey Stengel stepped up from the dugout and hollered, "Ruth, Gehrig, Huggins, *somebody* get that ball back to the infield!"

I don't think this was the precipitant leading to the eventual moving of the tributary markers, but it surely made sense to get it out of the way. Monument Park has become home to the immortalization of famous Yankees and is enclosed just beyond the left center field fence. Such names as Joe DiMaggio, Mickey Mantle, Roger Maris, Phil Rizzuto, Yogi Berra, Thurman Munson, Reggie Jackson, are a few of the baseball heroes honored with plaques, retired numbers, and monuments in this esteemed venue.

As a kid I didn't really follow baseball the game, but I had this inexplicable love of baseball cards. 1973 was my biggest collecting year, I think because I loved the far out colors Topps used and the bold graphics to illustrate the teams and such. This is how I began learning about the players of the day and some of those preceding. I have a little confession to make. I coveted the 1969 baseball cards of another. Little Marty was a teenager to my 9 year old self, and the son of my parent's best friends. He was hardly ever around when we were there, but I knew where he kept his collection in the basement, and sometimes I'd sneak a peek. Once, he gave me a couple of cards, which I completely treasured despite their unprestine raggedy appearance. I can still picture those cards clearly in my head, like the black and white action picture of Tom Seavers pitching in the '69 World Series for the New York Mets. Oh the hours of joy those cards provided, as I poured over them and built my collection.

The baseball cards led to my seeking autographs of players I found interesting. I'd sit at the table and write out a letter to the guy, telling him why I thought he was great, and put it in the mail. I'll remind you this was before the internet and eBay. I couldn't do an online search for addresses or bid on an available signed item; I put pen to paper and stamp to envelope. For Pete's sake, this was even when I had to do my own stamp licking rather than placing a self-adhesive one on. It was rough when I was a kid, but it was also great. I'd wait the few weeks and low and behold, an envelope would appear addressed to me. I garnered the signatures of such players as Yogi Berra, Vida Blue, and my most prized one even though I have no idea where it is today, I received an autographed picture of Hank Aaron.

1980 resurrected my baseball fascination with the Philadelphia Phillies being in and winning the World Series. I then lived just across the Delaware River in Marlton, New Jersey. We were practically a suburb of Philly, especially so since my father drove in every day to work. I remember Pete Rose starting the series by hitting off a dozen or more foul balls and finally getting on base. I thought at the time 'this is why I don't watch this game, it's boring,' but having become more learned about it now, I know what an amazing feat it was. Not to mention how it wears down a pitcher. Since then I have grown and moved to the far out skirts of Cleveland, Ohio, and lived the joys and misery of the Cleveland Indians. God, it's hard to be a Cleveland fan, and that goes for any and all professional sport associated with the city.

I've long since left behind collecting baseball cards. Hold up, that's not entirely true. Whenever Kim and I visit a city and go catch a ball game, I insist on making a trip to the stadium shop. For a few bucks I pick up the pre-packaged team's starting line-up, and all but do a happy dance when I have it in my hot little hand. Things have changed since I was nine when I would tear into the waxy paper packaging and extract the stick of stale bubblegum to endlessly peruse the cool cards I've acquired. Nowadays, I don't open up the cards, but just knowing I've got them is kind of my own tribute to the younger me. And now that I've revealed my own baseball history, maybe it explains my wanting to get into Yankee Stadium to check out theirs.

The perk of blindness with the granting of first entrance into Monument Park Was made even sweeter by the whole commotion Kim and I had gone through to get in at all. Excited and grateful, we skedaddled up the wheelchair ramp and all but hurled ourselves into Monument Park. Inside the enclosure, we began to figure out the lay of the land and Kim read this plaque and that sign. I'm telling you, Yankees history is not only long, it's abundant. They truly had the greats of the game. While Kim read, I would feel the engraved portraits of the plaques, or the raised sculpting of the monuments. It was an awesome tactile experience, especially when I got to the rounded cheeks of Babe Ruth. His entire face could be described as bulbous and it amused me greatly to give his cheek a pinch. Negotiating the area was somewhat difficult because of the sheer number of people crowded together, but Kim and I managed, and even did the picture taking thing.

Kim's discovery of a couple of special, unrelated to baseball, plaques grabbed our attention and interest. The first being the visit of Pope John Paul and the mass he conducted in Yankee Stadium. As any good baseball fan knows, some form of prayer and the use of God's name is frequently been invoked during a game, but I'm guessing the Pope's visit elicited a slightly different tone. At least I hope it did. The other plaque of distinction was dedicated to the individuals who lost their lives on September 11th, 2001. Many wonderful details of tribute were inscribed onto the plaque. Kim read it quietly, and even with the bustle and excited energy related to the game, we both were moved to a moment of silence.

Strolling as best as anyone can through a tightly confined crowded area, Kim and I thoroughly enjoyed reading and reminiscing about the Yankee legends. Yet my favorite part was still to happen. There was neither rhyme nor reason to our method of touring Monument Park; we ambled about until we came upon the wall overlooking the Yankee bullpen. Now this was cool and captivated my attention completely. There I stood, hanging over a bit and listened to the awesome sound of the pitched ball smacking into the catcher's mitt. There are so many great sounds associated with sports:

-   The trumpeted bugle calling the horses to their starting posts.
-   The rhythmic sound of a tennis ball in the midst of a volley as it goes from racquet to ground to racquet and back again.
-   The roll and thunderous crash of bowling ball upon pins as it performs a perfect strike.
-   The solid thump of foot upon pig skin as it sends it end over end through the uprights.
-   The swish of nothing but net in basketball.
-   The thwack of bat on ball sending it out of the park.

And right back to where I started, the ball sailing in at 90 miles an hour as it is gloved to a halt by the catcher.

I was filled with gleeful excitement as I stood listening to the pitcher's warm up. I stayed there for a while listening, until pushed out by the claustrophobic crowding of others wanting to have their own look-see. Stepping down from my perch, Kim led me around to what turned out to be the cushioned backstops of the bullpen. Only these two gigantic pillow-like contraptions separated me from those guys on the other side. The faintest thought fleeted through my overly active mind that maybe I could somehow squeeze through the crevice and get inside, but I swear it was just a nanno second of a notion. I never seriously entertained it. What idea did enter and stayed was that this very place,

Yankee Stadium, was soon to be torn down. I had joked about smuggling a chisel into the park and getting me a piece of the place, but eventually realized Kim was starting to worry I might go through with it. I'm capable of many things, but among them is not vandalism. Discrete thievery of the inane; that's another thing though. I composed myself as I stood this side of the bullpen and with my foot, I kind of coyly felt around in a hokey pokey-like manner. I put my foot in the bullpen, and then put it out. I stuck it in again, and moved it about. My antics led me to the discovery that I could with ease, hunker down, stick my hand in between the backstop cushions, and grab a bit of bullpen dirt. And that's exactly what I did.

Oh the ridiculous joy I felt as I stood holding clasped in my hand the dirt from Yankee Stadium's bull pen. It was all good as I stuck my crumbled bits into my shorts pocket, later to be salvaged and bagged ever so carefully. Kim was just relieved I wasn't caught and gotten us into trouble. To be quite honest, I think she's getting use to me and my lunatic behavior. If it had come to it though, I think she would have left my ass with the police and still taken in the game before bailing me out. Fortunately that'll never be known, because neither was my dirt snatchery.

We finished our perusal of Monument Park and felt extremely grateful to the stadium gent who originally nixed the rule wanting to keep us out. Kim attempted to locate this good man so we could once again extend our gratitude, but he was nowhere to be found. As far as I'm concerned, he was truly our angel in the outfield, and Kim and I soon learned just how much the Bronx was brimming with good hearted types.

Promised kept, Kim and I headed for our bleacher seat assignments after our visit to Monument Park—and the gift shop. C'mon, it was right there on the way out, so it technically doesn't count as doing anything but leaving, as we originally said we'd do. Kim and I both noticed the energy of the excited crowd outside the stadium as we weaved our way towards our designated entry gate. We took the opportunity to stop into a couple of stores, and enjoyed chats with clerks brandishing their very distinct New York styled accents and personalities. Being at Yankee

Stadium was much more than just watching a baseball game; it was a festive show that started hours before the first pitch was thrown.

Legitimately getting in this time, Kim and I decided it would be best to load up on the necessities before finding our seats. A couple of hot dogs, soda in gigantic souvenir cups, and a tray of cheesy nachos, were easily paid for by a second mortgage taken out on our house. We were all set to belch our way through the game and see the Yankees play ball.

Our little section of Yankee Stadium was an add-on back in the 70's. There was nothing glamorous about it, and to be completely truthful, there wasn't much to be said for the stadium in general. Dingy and old would be the kinder, gentler descriptions used, giving supported evidence to the idea for a new Yankee home. Yet it was this very nostalgia and history that made this park great. I imagine the millions of people who over the eight decades of the stadiums existence had done what I was doing right now. Although better dressed, at least in those early days, fans of the game would find their seats, munch on a hot dog, and get ready to see their heroes play. It's hard to believe that the everyday Joe or Josephine back in the day would dress in suit or heels, and always wear a properly placed hat. We've evolved in our clothing style from suit-able attire, to casual becoming the preferred norm. As with the change in people, their clothes, the game itself, I guess it may be time for a change in venue, although I would personally find it very difficult if I were a home grown fan. I understand why a person falls in love with inanimate objects; this very place is certainly among the most beloved. Tradition, by-gone days and people, and the great game of baseball, America's past time, all embodied in this iconic establishment known as Yankee Stadium. And, here we were.

THE GAME

Saddled on the metal seats of the bleachers and ready for the game to start, Kim and I did some observing before the first pitch. It was a beautiful night for baseball, and the house was packed. I felt as though we were amongst friends seated in the bleachers, thanks partly to tight accommodations, and more because of the four fellas sitting behind us. It quickly became obvious this was a man's night without the wives, especially since they said as much. No better broadcasters could there be than these guys. Between there knowledgeable commentary, enthusiasm for the game, and colorful New York colloquialisms, I was having a blast listening in. They knew I was doing it too because subtle I am not, but they never seemed to mind my eaves dropping and the occasional questions I had of them.

Home field advantage has probably been documented statistically somewhere along the way, but I'd rather focus on home field antics. The game of baseball has always been meant to be a spectator sport, I mean really, how far would it have gotten if nobody was watching in the first place. And despite my affection for the game, I can still understand how some might perceive it to be slow, boring, or the equivalent of watching grass grow. Baseball has recognized this, although not openly admitting to this perception, and has over the years incorporated ways to entertain the fans between at bats, innings, and so on. From the early use of organs inciting the crowd to charge, to team mascots dancing on the dugout, to flashy computered graphically enhanced scoreboards, Major League Baseball has evolved into an entertainment industry for the ADHD fan of today. I may have come across as a little cynical there, so let me see if I can tone down my rhetoric and share the traditions of the game I found endearing at Yankee Stadium.

There we sat, Kim and me in the bleacher section of Yankee Stadium, speaking nary a word to each other for a while. We were taking it all in, each in our own way of course. Kim is an incredibly visual person. I'm sure her big browns were dancing as they laid on all there was to see. Me, I did what I do; I listened and absorbed the sounds surrounding us. It's an awesome thing to hear thousands of people gathered together, and when they all commence to cheering, well; sometimes it could be described as heavenly—unless you're an opponent to the thing being cheered. I was completely amused by the fans as the starting lineup was being announced. It seems each Yankee has his own tailored made response by the cheering crowd, my favorite being that of Gorge Posada, and "Hip Hip Gorge!"

As I listened to the PA announcer doing his thing, I couldn't help but notice the guy sounded, how shall I say, really, really old. I pointed him out to Kim making some kind of smart-aleck remark pondering if he announced the first game when the stadium opened in 1923. Not till later did I learn about the "Voice of Yankee Stadium", Bob Sheppard. Since 1951, which isn't all that far from 1923, Mr. Sheppard has been introducing players in his distinct manner. Imagine this, in his very first game with the Yankees he announced the names of Joe DiMaggio, Mickey Mantle, Johnny Mize, Yogi Berra, and Phil Rizzuto from the Yankee line up. And since they were playing the Boston Red Sox, he also happened to throw in Ted Williams and Lou Boudreau. These seven players in one game on Bob Sheppard's first day of work all just happen to be future Hall of Famers. Now, fifty-seven years later, Mr. Sheppard called out the names, position, and number from the likes of Alex Rodriguez and Derek Jeter, quite likely hall of famers in the making.

The Yankee establishment does a fine job of walking the line by keeping tradition and incorporating some of today's expectations. The music of a live organ being played to energize the fans, and the use of pre-recorded music for each player coming to the plate combines past with present. Having the "Voice of Yankee Stadium" announce the players, while displaying graphics and re-plays on the scoreboard, further brings the game to life. The tradition of standing in the 7th inning for not only a stretch and a rousing chorus of "Take Me Out to the Ball Game" have been made poignant with the addition of singing "God Bless America", which began in the days following September 11th.

It was all good. The atmosphere, the perfect June night, and the Bronx boys behind us, what more could any out-of-towner want from a ball game. How about a home team victory?! The New York Yankees pummeled the San Diego Padres in an 8-nothing romp. Kim, the Padres, and I all learned about the "Power of the Stache" when Jason Giambi smacked a couple of homers out of the park. I'll clarify for you as it was done for me. The "stache" refers to the fuzzy growth betwixt Giambi's nose and upper lip. I tell you, baseball folk will grab hold of anything if it puts runs up on the board, and apparently this magical mustache has just such ability. Not to be completely outdone, A Rod contributed his very own homerun, while Mariano Rivera, one of the greatest closers ever, finished things up by striking out the side. It was a fantastic game to witness, made only better by the stadium tradition of playing Frank Sinatra's "new York new York" after the win.

THE BRONX BLUES

It was a quintessential New York night with the smooth styling of Sinatra, Yankee fans spilling into the streets celebrating a win, and Kim and I at the mercy of the fates, better known in this case as cabbies.

Part of our original trip plan always involved taking a taxi after the game, and this intention remained, however it was the execution of it that gave us problems. Distance was never the issue, rather the Bronx nightfall and the mind set of strangers in a strange land elicited concerned pause from us both. We wandered up to and were repeatedly rejected by cabbies wanting a more substantial fair. Each waved us on to the next as we circumnavigated the stadium in search of a ride. By the way, the stereotype of cab drivers being of foreign origin held very true in our experience, and words were not so much exchanged as were negating grunts and a hand gesture or two. The last taxi driver we approached responded in kind and motioned us across the street. At the time we interpreted his meaning as "go look over there". However, from the vantage of hindsight, I've since wondered if he simply meant the hotel was just over that-away. Now standing on the other side of the street and not a single cab in sight, we were at a loss for what to do.

I proposed we chance it and hightail ourselves back to the hotel, but Kim's self preserving tendencies took over and she would have nothing to do with my idea and rightfully so. Even putting safety issues aside, it would've been nuts for us to attempt a hotel find in the dark, much less in a place completely unfamiliar to us, especially considering our track record. Whether the appearance of indecision and frustration, or simply the obvious look of a couple of tourists lost, factored into what occurred next, I can only surmise.

Standing there fervently communicating amongst our own selves, we were interrupted by a kindly Bronx police officer. Politely he inquired,

"Are you looking for something?" Brother, were we ever. I quickly conveyed our dilemma, and asked if it would be safe for us to walk it back to the hotel. I think Mr. Officer took one look at the two of us, remembered his sworn oath to protect and serve, as well as his strong dislike for paperwork generated by crimes perpetuated on the innocent such as ourselves, or would that be the ignorant, and decided to have a chat with his partner. Moments later he was back and escorting us to a police cruiser, having worked things out for his partner to give us a lift.

Kim's fears now arrested, she climbed happily into the back of the police car. I made myself at home riding shotgun with Ms. Officer and resisted the urge to play with the buttons controlling the siren. My imaginings had me right in the middle of a NYPD Blue episode as I listened to our New York accented host and heard the chatter coming over the radio. Lights a flashing and the single whoop blasted from the siren when going left of center to leave all the traffic to the common folks, made this three minute joy ride along a memory to last a lifetime. Cruising with one of New York's finest was an awesome thrill. Not only was it unexpected in showing us the softer side of the blue, but it really got us out of an unpleasant pickle. Dropped at the hotel entrance, Kim and I practically fell over ourselves thanking our wonderful police woman for her kindnesses and for such a cool experience.

Obviously the actions of these police officers were well outside the realm of their normal duties. We could easily have been sent on our way, but these officers from the 50th Precinct, their thoughtfulness and consideration for our well-being, have left Kim and me with tremendous respect and gratitude. So I say thank you to those good police people who went out of their way to uphold the serve portion of the creed, and did so with friendliness and kindness.

Our incredible New York night was over, but this story isn't yet finished. We still had to get out of the Bronx the following morning. Thank goodness we slept well for what we were about to put ourselves through.

Rising to the shine of a beautiful summer sky, and still in the glow from all the good fortunes of the night before, Kim and I didn't want to dawdle the day away. We checked out and decided to pick up a paper as we left. Back in my mother's car and GPS all fired up, we rolled out onto the Bronx streets.

If we weren't looking for a newspaper there would have been a paper dispensing box or newsstand on every corner. But since this was our departing mission, we couldn't find a thing. After circling around for a while, we eventually stumbled on what appeared to be a mom and pop shop. You know, it would be an interesting sociological study to chart the progression of ownership of these stores in correlation to the changing times of American immigration. I had automatically assumed mom and pop to be of western European heritage and accent, but as we entered the doors, I learned my pre-conceived mindset was wrong. The parental persons owning this particular establishment appeared to be of Indian origin. Paper in hand and touting the big Yankee win, Kim and I headed back to our borrowed car from my mom.

On our drive up to the city, Kim had left all settings alone on my mother's car. Even though her arms were a bit out stretched, she managed the drive rather comfortably. For whatever reason came into Kim's head, she decided for the trip back to make a few adjustments to her accommodations. Mom's car is one of those foreign filled gadget automobiles, while Kim is more use to the basic model of transportation. A non-bell and whistle gal, she prefers individual efforting to put windows up and make adjustments to mirrors, seats, and such. For Pete's sake, Kim doesn't even have a light in the trunk of her car. So when she placed her finger to that first button and gave it a push, Kim knew not the effects it would cause.

Button pressed, the seat hummed as the electric generated the motor into action and propelled both Kim and her seat forward—and forward still. And even further forward until Kim's chest pressed smashingly against the driver's wheel. Legs now folded under the column, her knees were quite able to reach both gas and brake pedals if need be, Kim observantly stated, "This isn't going to work." Seeking out the counter button to her current predicament, Kim pressed yet another one and felt the driver chair gyrate and contort into another position. The result, Kim was now angled in a downward slope and still firmly embedded into the steering wheel.

My efforts to silence the laughter welling inside me became futile as Kim grunted and groaned her dismay. Each click of a button evoked seating changes and sounds of discontentment from the thoroughly smashed Kim. For a moment hoped soared when the key was removed from the ignition and all retreated back a bit, but it was soon crushed, along with Kim, when the key was replaced and returned her to her awkward positioning.

I couldn't help myself, God knows I really tried, but I erupted with laughter. Tears flowed freely down my cheeks as I convulsed with hysteria. Any one of you would've been doing the same if you were there. I'd hear the click of a button, the hum of seat movement, and the arghing of Kim as she was smooshed once again. In an effort to be a better person, I gained some control of myself and got out of the car to offer my assistance. Unfortunately, I did no better and actually had to step away for a moment to keep from having a bladder malfunction.

I'd like to say Kim was having as much fun as I was, but if it wasn't already obvious to me, it surely became so when profanity was utilized to describe the car she was now trapped in. I made a 911 call to my mother, seeking guidance after a brief description of the predicament, and Kim's mental status. It was to no avail, for the directions given from an entire state away, changed nothing. Resigning herself to the four hour trip home plastered to the steering wheel was not easy, but neither was stifling the laughter I kept held in.

Picture this. One Kim Shepard driving a borrowed luxury car squished and hunched over the steering wheel, in the middle of the Bronx, with a blind co-pilot, while listening to a navigational device giving directions, during rush hour. Sounds wonderful don't it. As bad as imagined, it was even worse in reality. This was one of those times you dream about and wake from in a cold sweat. There was traffic everywhere and following the GPS directions resulted in a wrong turn at a no turn intersection.

The joy of lights and sirens experienced the night before became but a distant memory as we heard them this time in a whole new context.

Pulled over and waiting for the police officer to approach the car, Kim confessed, "I've never been so relieved to see a cop." Not the typical response to being stopped, but considering everything, it made sense. Kim viewed this as another Bronx rescue and immediately planned on asking the officer to direct us out. Pegged as out-of-towners, Mr. Policeman did his job and then some. Making a potentially stressful situation humorous, he quickly realized we weren't hardened criminals thumbing our noses at the law, rather instead, two very confused gals lost in the big city. He offered up directions unsolicited, and even stopped traffic both ways directing Kim to make a U turn which would take us to the George Washington Bridge, and Jersey. Maybe if I was going to be cynical, I'd think he probably did all this because he wanted us gone from his jurisdiction as quickly as possible, but I'm sure it was just because he was another one of the good guys in blue. And as we drove off, Kim realized she should have asked our latest knight in shining armor to fix the stupid car seat; Opportunity missed, Kim's intimate relationship with my mother's car remained intact all the way home.

IT'S A WONDERFUL TOWN

Although hospitality is typically assigned to all things southern, I would offer our own experiences to strongly make the case for its existence in New York City. The kindness of strangers was overwhelming to us and I have often spoken of it since. I am grateful to have encountered all those wonderful people who have enriched not only the time we spent in New York, but our lives as well. I encourage all of you to visit this great city filled to over flowing with history, the arts, variety of cultures, tastes, music, and boy, how the list could go on from there. My recent adventures barely skimmed the surface of a city suffering from insomnia. Therefore, I say without hesitation, watch out New York; I'll be back.

SITES UNSEEN TIPS

LET YOUR FINGERS DO THE SEEING

Sometimes, the sighted folks just don't get how visual the blind can be. I know, that sounded a tad paradoxical, or is it oxymoronic? Either way, it makes sense to me, because we too have the need to see things, at least in our own way. I've already spoken of using my mind's eye, my imagination to enhance the experience of a site unseen. Now I want to point out the multi-purposed index finger. This single digit not only can permit the blind to read in the dark, but it also is capable of providing perspective.

In my travels, I often want to envision what others are beholding, and I have discovered how simply this can be achieved by the use of my finger. As I described back at the ball game and at Ground Zero, Kim has taken my index finger and used it to trace the outline of the image wanting to be seen. This simple act allows me to conjure up the size, shape, distance, height, or whatever else I might want to figure out. Additionally, the finger is a ready-made writing utensil and has helped me comprehend designs, graphics, and a variety of writings used in the big world. Handily, the finger is always with me, so whipping it out and seeing things my way is right there at my fingertips.

3D POSTCARDS

I had been doing it for years, but didn't know what it was until I couldn't see any more. I'm talking about the acquisition of my 3D postcards. All those years I thought I was just purchasing travel mementos, but in reality, I was furthering my tactile need to see. And again, the mighty mind machine continues to rationalize her OCD collector habit. It's a gift.

Speaking of gifts, the best way to more accurately comprehend a site you want to see is by visiting the local tourist gift shop. Whether you actually purchase the item is your own business, but at the very least, go have a feel of the miniaturized monument, structure, or landmark you are visiting. It's a great way to see it. If I happen to be somewhere like the Statue of Liberty and can easily recall her appearance, I might wait until after the visit to peruse the souvenir stand. But if it's something I don't have stowed away in my memory, I purposefully go first to the trinkets to get it into my head.

As for my 3D postcard collection at home, I proudly display them as would anyone framing a picture and placing it on the wall. It is my own tactile gallery providing wonderful memories and a sense of achievement.

RELATING DIRECTIONS

Here is a little guide tip review. It seems the most commonly known technique to assist a person with vision limitations is the use of hand positions on a clock. Everyone knows where the 3:00, 6:00, 9:00, 12:00 directions are on the clock face, so using these positions are universal. However, all this gets screwed up if the guide and the guided are not in sync. For example, say each are sitting across the table from one another, what is 12:00 for one becomes 6:00 for the other. The guide will often consider this and make the proper adjustments in relating the time positions correctly. Remember, directions are always to be given from the vantage point of the person needing the directions—in other words, the guided.

I gave the simplest of examples already; however making adjustments with directions isn't always that easy. A little helpful hint I'd like to provide the person doing the guiding is to think about where's the belly button on the individual you are with. Yep, the belly button. This anatomical feature is a constant. No matter which way the person is turned, twisted, or facing, the belly button will always be in the 12:00 position. Feet, eyes, or any other body part could be any which a way, but the naval, it ain't going nowhere else. All numerical directions then should be from this vantage point. A quick review of these facts with both members of the guiding team will make the communicating and understanding of directions a breeze.

3

CHICAGO, ILLINOIS

There are many reasons to travel, yet only once in a while will pure inspiration lead the way. Our plans to visit the Windy City herself, Chicago, were the result of Kim's genius. An avid runner for more than a decade, Kim has beaten the streets with her rubbered soles of every place we have gone. Usually the run is the byproduct of a trip; however the plan to go to Chicago was the motivation this time.

The proposal to make plans went something very similar to this. It was a cold winter's night as I lay hunkered down under the blankets readying myself for sleep. The hour was super late, around ten o'clock, when Kim said in an excited tone, "I want to run in the Chicago Gay Games." My muffled pillowed response was not unlike "That's nice dear," which was good enough for Kim to take as agreement. Not until the following day did I have the where with all to ask a few follow up questions, the primary being, what on earth is the Gay Games anyway? I'll explain this more in a moment, but first let's talk about our destination.

The toddlin' town of Chicago truly is second to none. Influential beyond its Midwest boundaries, the ever changing city sits upon the shores of the mighty Lake Michigan. Only the hearty would have the gumption to proclaim its harsh blustery ways of weather a beloved nickname, and yet adopt "Urbs in Horto", as its delicate motto meaning city in a park. Chi-town's streets and neighborhoods are as varied and colorful as its history, of which all have greatly played a part in the development of culture, industry, and, dare I say it, politics. From the legend of a clumsy cow setting the city afire, to the very real gangsters bootlegging their way around the laws of Prohibition, Chicago's stories are the stuff

Laura E. Walker

from which good movies are made. More than any other trait, it's the people who have journeyed to and made Chicago home that I find to be the wonders of this city. Whether it was the Great Migration of the African-Americans of the south, the countless immigrants seeking a new way of living, or those who grew up for generations within its limits, all have placed their mark on a city with the biggest and best of shoulders.

Kim and I knew this trip to Chicago was going to be an opportunity of a lifetime and decided it had to be shared. It was a must do for my darling daughter Sarah who at the ripe old age of thirteen had already exhibited her affinity for big city visiting. But who could we invite along that we liked well enough to spend a few days? Oh how easily the answer came by the way of our gal pals Nancy, Frannie, and the mighty Jud B. These awesome women are some of the best people I have ever had the privilege of knowing. Once idolized, I have taken them off of the pedestal and have them all squarely in the friend-family place in my heart; Kim has firmly dittoed this sentiment. An invitation was extended, everyone said yes, and Kim and I happy-danced with excitement.

WHAT AND HOW

Let's take care of a couple of "what'chu talkin' about Willis" items, in case you haven't already figured it out yet. Firstly, I have her permission, so I'm just going to say it. Kim's gay. Yep, that innocent faced, feminine, make-up wearing, purse toting lady is a lesbian. Has been for a while now, kind of like her whole life. No choice about it even, well maybe a little bit when she did the whole "date guys thing", but other than that it's just the way she is. Oh, and for the record, so am I. Minus the make-up and purse shi . . . stuff. I did a little choosing my own self too, sixteen married years of it, but it was one of the best choices I ever made since I am privileged to be my baby girl's mom.

Our orientation officially outed; I'll address my earlier proposed question of, "What on earth are the Gay Games?" It's a celebration of a people and their culture. The purpose of the Gay Games is to recognize achievement and honor all inclusively, not exclusively. There are no requirements to enter, no time trials, eliminating events, only the allowance of proud participation. The very idea of celebrating gay culture via the use of athletics without the nuisance of competition, was more than appealing; it was inviting. As with the international Olympics, the Gay Games occur every four years and are held in a different city around the world. Kim and I decided with the games being practically in our own backyard, and this possibly the only chance we'd get to go, we had to be a part of it with our friends.

Regarding the hows—as in the hows we getting there and hows we goin' to manage this—two words set the course, practicality and economy. This trip needed to be cost friendly since our group was made up of quasi retirees, a social worker, receptionist, and a kid. Upon securing accommodations, we had only the task of figuring out how to get there and quite literally explored planes, trains, and automobiles. The pros and cons all weighed, the economic winner became a minivan rental. It may have been a six-hour trip to and from Chicago in really close quarters, but traveling with the likes of these women made time seem irrelevant. Conversation flowed as easily as the silent moments. Each of us found comfortable niches to call our own; Jud B. in the hole, Frannie or Kim driving, Nancy taking over as navigator, and Sarah and I occupying the mid-section of the vehicle.

The drive into Chicago was as smooth as it comes, until urban road construction reared its ugly head. The clever advertisers of the red line public transit took advantage of the captive bumper to bumper traffickers and provided a whole host of clever signs to point out their thwarted progress. My favorite queried, "Are you seeing RED yet?" It got a good round of laughter from the group as we inched by.

The first mission in town was to deposit Kim at the Hilton for registration purposes. Entrance found with relative ease, we kicked Kim to the curb and proceeded on to our hotel. Sticking with the miserly plan of tourism, we all agreed to pile into one room, request a cot and min frig, and hope for the best. And that is exactly what we got. Imagine our thrill to discover a spacious room awaiting us. It took a bit for us to put all the puzzle pieces together regarding our generous digs, but we did eventually assemble the clues. We had a ginormous bathroom with grips all over the place, a door peephole peering right about crotch level, and so much room in the room, a semi-truck could've driven through. I'll be blatant about it, with me getting us checked in, we were given the designated disability accommodations and got us some mighty fine livin' quarters. The perks of blindness are bountiful and apparently sizable too.

Ordinarily fitting six people into one hotel room might be cumbersome and cramped, yet thankfully it was not at this fine establishment. Roll-away bed procured for Jud B, the two couples declared squatter's rights on the full sized beds, and Sarah made herself a wonderful little nest on the floor. Don't go feeling sorry for the kid, with plenty of room, lots of blankets to keep her comfy, and a conveniently placed window ledge that doubled as a shelf to neatly stack books and DVDs, she had herself a perfect little pad to call her own.

Organization was the key to being in close quarters, so the Queen of that department, Nancy, immediately took matters into hand. Innovation and adaptation led the way. Most common folk would look at a hotel room safe, laugh about the idea of having anything worth locking up, and leave the thing alone for the rest of their stay. Not this crew, Frannie suggested the safe be used much like a pantry and Nancy was all over it, neatly stacking supplies. When food storage was needed, we trusted our safe with these precious belongings.

Meanwhile, and not to be outdone, Jud B created her own economical use of space. Roll-away stashed into a corner, pillows continually migrated onto her bed, allowing Jud B her very own fortress of solitude. Taking a lesson from the safe pantry, she stowed her gear below this mattress on wheels and declared it to be her crawl in closet. I still laugh now thinking about Jud B on her knees rummaging under her bed as I nearly tripped over her trying to get to the bathroom. We scared each other senseless. I was thinking an animal somehow got into the room as my hand landed on her fuzzy head and Jud B with the vision of being crushed to smithereens by a pee-filled blind woman.

I wish I could say I had something to contribute to all this hub bub, but I didn't. Instead I admired the ingenuity of the group and applauded while providing positive feedback. The simple unpacking of my belongings into a drawer and my keeping out of the way was the best I had to offer, for now.

SOLDIERING ON

All neatly nested into our burrow, it was time for our tribe to make tracks and catch up with Kim again. Because of her athletic responsibilities, namely registering and getting to the opening ceremonies site, we hadn't seen the gal since we left her on a street corner hours ago.

Negotiating Chicago's streets during rush hour is not the best way to take in the city, but we weren't aiming to do this anyway. All that our group wanted was to get from our hotel down to Soldier Field, and really, how difficult could that be with the extensive transit system Chicago has to offer? Plenty of time presented itself to ponder this very question on the bus, as we advanced at the rip roaring speed of 10 FPM, feet per minute, and made the slow crawl down to the stadium.

Packed in unmercifully tight, I became all too familiar with the local city workers and the nature of their business. Not so much eavesdropping as having my head spoken through, I listened to the close talkers plastered on my person. Fortunately these individuals using the bus at this alleged hurried hour are well groomed for their employment, so the cramp quartered intimacy of our transportation remained bearable. In what seemed like forever, we finally came near enough to Soldier Field for Nancy to see it in the distance and urge us off this infernal contraption. We would make our final approach on foot.

More than a leisurely pace set to cover ground, we joined in with fellow opening ceremony seekers. Falling into stride and whipping out her video camera, Jud B took to her self-ascribed role as the woman on the street. Accosting complete strangers with her dynamo style of interviewing, Jud B relished the opportunity to let film role. Innocent passer-byers were queried on their reasons for being present, where they hailed from, as well as their general thoughts and feelings about the Gay Games.

No gay event would be complete without the obligatory protestors, and as anticipated, those nay-sayers were Johnny on the spots. It has almost become comical with the fundamental bull horned blowharding, yet there is truly nothing amusing about the attempt to incite hatred and spread bigotry, and in the name of God—what the hell? I'll be honest; my concern regarding these people vehemently espousing anti-gay tirades was always for Sarah. I was afraid she would be hurt by the ugly words directed at me, her mother, and the people she knew. Extolling the sage wisdom of a thirteen year old, Sarah simply said, "They're stupid." This ability to ignore the ignorant has seemingly spread, for the vast crowds simply walked on by, paying them no never mind.

Some distance walked, and a variety of people passed, we eventually hoofed it up to the entry gates of Soldier Field. Once there, our group collectively turned to the obvious ticket carrying choice of Nancy with her multi-pocketed, velcroed-shut, shorts. Poised in receipt readiness, we waited.

It's amazing how silence can be telling, and right then, it was speaking volumes. I didn't have to observe Nancy patting herself down as she searched each and every pocket on her person. I didn't need to see the expression on her face changing from idle "huh", to that of "oh shit" as realization washed over her with the tickets gone. I could feel the vibe mild panic elicits, and rather than giving into it, our wonderful little group rallied. As is so often the case with good friends, when one feels bad, we all feel the pain. Reassurances are genuinely given, ideas lead to problem solving and action. Available money pooled, Nancy and I back tracked to find a scalper with some tickets and got the five we needed.

Crossing the gated threshold, I chuckled to myself about the versatility of Soldier Field. Originally constructed in the 1920's, the horseshoe shaped stadium has undergone a couple of extreme makeovers, varying its appearance nearly as much as its capacity. The one time seating of a quarter million Catholics, pales in comparison to today's configuration of a mere sixty-one thousand rabid football fans. Sports have also run the gambit with track and field, boxing, soccer, a brief NASCAR stint, and since the 1970's, home turf of the Chicago Bears football team. From the incredible rally of the Chicago Freedom Movement with Dr. Martin Luther King Jr. as its speaker, to the rockin' good times in concerts by Bruce Springsteen and the final Grateful Dead performance, Soldier Field has played host to a wide variety of events. As I walked the ramp leading to our seats, I couldn't help but think the Field founders probably never had this in mind, the ultimate fabulousness of the Gay Games opening ceremony.

Continually ascending, our gang climbed the stairway into the heavens, or better known in arena talk as the nosebleed seats. Our vantage point allowed a body, or five sets of peepers, to see the lay of the land. This worked for us, because as we sat there well past the original gig start time, the abled eyes took note of available empty seats below. Section by section we descended into open seating until we landed on the same level we were supposed to be with our first set of tickets. We were ready for the big show to begin and all excited with anticipation.

THE GRAND GAYLA

The pulsing energy filling Soldier Field was palpable. The very air, electric. Thousands of spectators from around the world gathered in this place and awaited the start of something promising to be spectacular. The opening ceremony of the VII Gay Games would set into motion a week long celebratory event. Readied in our newly acquired seats, our little cheer squad surged with the same energy that had over taken our surroundings. It had been hours since we last saw our representative athlete, Kim, and the expectations of spotting her amongst the fanfare was beyond exciting.

Unbridled hoopla went up when the announcers welcomed everyone, and was virtually unending as the athletes took the field. As in the opening ceremony at the Olympics, each country entered the stadium alphabetically, and had designated athletes carrying signs and country flags. More than 11,000 athletes took to the field representing 65 countries in all. Thunderous applause of support was given regardless of affiliation, and became incredibly poignant when a solitary member representing an oppressed African nation marched proudly onto the field. Some athletes literally risked their lives to participate in the

Games due to the on-going persecution of gay individuals remaining in the world. This brave soul was one of these people. The standing ovation and cheers of unity clearly showed he was among friends.

Having the home field advantage always means the ability to participate is greater, and this held true when the American contingency came marching in. The booming announcement of the United States of America evoked tremendous cheers, and continued as state by state the athletes poured out onto the field. Our group rose collectively to our feet with the O's drawing near, saving ourselves a bit until Ohio was announced. Screaming at the top of my lungs, or as best as I could since I became choked with emotion, I let my people know how proud of them I truly was. I was overcome with this feeling and the ultimate declaration of acceptance. I imagined my Kim down there, out of her mind with all the flashing camera lights, the multitudes exhibiting their excitement, and the unadulterated joy of being in it all. As I teared up and shouted out to the Ohio delegation somewhere in the sea of people before me, the ably eyed watched the big screen to catch a glimpse of Kim and her pony tailed self running onto the stadium floor.

Later, Kim recounted the entire experience of standing behind the curtain waiting to be announced. The organizer pumping them up and yelling, "Are you ready Ohio?" And being released with exhortations to "go go go!" She went went went, her feet barely touching the ground as she was carried by the sheer emotion of it all. The overwhelming feeling of elation Kim experienced was more than her tear ducts could manage as her large doe eyes brimmed over. I'm of the mindset that everyone should have a moment such as this in their lives. One where each person is being accepted, supported, and cheered for being themselves, and then capturing this moment in memory to relive over and over. How much better would we all be as a people if this could be done?

Athletes entered Soldier Field first by country, then by state, and finally the city of Chicago got its own spot in the processional. Bursting from the tunnel, they flowed forth nearly endlessly. Undoubtedly the largest contingency represented, the Chicagoans came close to matching the rest of the world in its size. With the final participants stepping into place on the field, the athlete's and participant's oath was recited by former professional football running back David Kopay. Upon conclusion, the stadium fell into darkness. There before us was a wonderful rainbow of color created by the athletes themselves wearing lighted glow sticks. Cheers of approval lifted from the audience as the athletes waved and wiggled in response.

All stops were pulled in getting big wigs to the party and began with the official welcoming by Mayor Richard Daily. His speech was politically crafted, yet sincere in delivery when speaking to the need for open acceptance of all people. Dignitaries having had their platform, it was time for festivities and entertainment. Some well knowns were enlisted to be part of the show, like Megan Mullally from Will and Grace, George Takei of Star Trek, Jodi Whatley the singer, and comedians Kate Clinton and Margaret Cho. Others performed but I hadn't a clue who they were. To be brutally honest, I was rather confused by the esoteric, unique, how shall I say, weird things taking place on that field. Lest I sound judgmental, I'll just say not all forms of artistic expression are my cup of tea, but good on them for getting out there and doing it.

Kim joined us in the stands after tracking us down via cell phone, and girl howdy, was she flying high. I guess adoration and adulation of thousands could do that to some. Of course our response to seeing her again with all the hugging and "atta girls" given might have factored in too. All I know is she beamed with happiness, and I, for her.

All together again, we took in the showy opening ceremony, at least for as long as we could. After three hours of it, plus everything else we did in getting here this day, it seemed the distant sound of our beds calling us was overpowering. Here's where it gets complicated though. Some of us wanted to go, while an equal amount wanted to stay. The first grouping was Frannie, Sarah, and I, and not needing approval or consensus, we headed out to find the bus home. Shortly after our departure, the rest of the gang decided they had had enough and followed suit. I don't know how it happened, or why it had to happen to us, but we, seeking sleep first returned to the hotel last. Sitting on a bus stop bench forever, we most likely and literally watched the rest of them pass us by. Nothing wanted to stop and take us away, and it's still a mystery how we ended up wherever we did waiting for the blasted bus. One day rolling into the next, our bedraggled little trio managed to get back, but not to bed. The other gals had found a twenty-four hour McDonald's with ice cream, and that cold life sustaining dairy product trumped sleep, as always.

RUN KIMMY RUN!

The idea of being Kim's cheer entourage seemed a mighty fine one when we all agreed to do it several months earlier, but sure was a lousy one when the alarm rang out at three-ish in the morning. Cutting into our already short night, the grouped groaned into a semi-wakeful state and began the readying process. Kim's presence was required clear on the other side of town by 5:00AM. The offered explanation given for this ridiculous earliness, running before the heat of the day, was understandable even for this non-runner type, but made it no easier to separate self from bed.

I believe there was a certain pang of guilt Kim felt as we stretched and stumbled about like sleep deprived zombies. She suggested we all stay in bed, and Nancy put it out there best when she said, "Kim, we're here because of you." In fact, we were, and the cheer posse echoed the sentiment. I could feel Kim's soul smile as her heart lightened from the loving support.

Here it was our first morning in Chicago and we were roaming the streets even before the sun. Brows quickly began to glisten with sweat from the thick summer humidity, our only reprieve, solar rays hadn't brought it to a boil. The city morning song played out upon the buses, as creaking metal and hydraulic doors released to gather in its passengers. The urban darkness glowed from the light provided by a store front sign and the occasional street lamp. Our surroundings felt desolate to me, as if no one else occupied the city but us, and for a moment my blind eye and ample imaginings placed us in a post-apocalyptic Chicago.

A moist chill sat on the air as we trekked along sidewalks to the bus stop. Exact change fished out of pockets, our intrepid group of six climbed aboard the bus. I immediately noticed the difference of five in the morning busing compared to that of five in the afternoon; with ample seating and the bus cruising along unimpeded. Kim's excitement grew as we drew nearer to our destination, and by the time we joined other participants on the shores of Lake Michigan, we were all feeling enthused with our adventure. Oh sure, we wanted coffee, a bit of breakfast, but more than that, we wanted to be there for Kim.

As Kim readied herself for the race with the obligatory stretching and jumping runners do to limber up, she wore a specially designed t-shirt donning the Liberation United Church of Christ name. Wonderful sentiments of support from our church family covered it, and Kim. Lined up, athletes at their marks, the gun signaled the racers into motion for the 10K run. Off Kim went with LIBERATION plastered proudly across her back and a rainbow of blessings patting her with encouragement. The rest of us standing on the sidelines whooped with cheers as our champion smiled from ear to ear.

The next fifty-some minutes allowed us to visit with the other supporters, talk amongst ourselves, and receive the occasional phone call from Kim updating us on her whereabouts on the course. She has this habit of doing a little site seeing while on a run and can hardly contain herself with a good find. I always wait for it, knowing my Kim the way I do, and she never fails to deliver. Phones connected, I hear her heavy breathing as she relays what famous building she might be near, a cool sign someone has made, something pretty she sees, or any other item catching her fancy. This is just one of the adorable traits that makes Kim easy to love. Kim's never alone on a race either, because her cheer team is always just a phone call away.

Some of the more earnest non-site seeing runners began crossing the finish line. Unwilling to resist, we got all caught up in their celebration and personal victory. It seems cheering is quite infectious. Once started for someone, it was only deserving for the next runner to receive encouragement as well. So the clapping and shouts continued for all who accomplished their goal. Not too much later, a Kimmy sighting was made, and gave way to the loudest cheers and the chant "KIM-MY KIM-MY"! Thrusting her hands high in victory as she crossed the finish line, our jubilant and incredibly sweaty Kim reveled in the welcome and the glory of it all.

MILLENIUM PARK

10K completed and Kim re-hydrated it was soon realized it was barely seven o'clock in the morning. An entire day lay before us so the decision to think on its doings over breakfast was a natural one. Thing is, we were somewhere over thatta-way, when we really wanted to be yonder. The only way to fix it was by hopping yet another bus. I've been on many kinds of buses in my day. I ride one to work. I've taken the doubled decker variety both with and without roofs. I've been on the luxurious sort accommodating distance travelers. And of course, I have experienced the spine crunching joys of a school bus as well. But this time I was going to shake, rattle, and roll a whole new way.

Totally not related to the Games, instead to an opportunity in merriment, our band of Chicago wanderers continued on to the unknown waiting for us. I have often spoken of the simple small things in life which can be the source of some of the most fun, laughter, and maker of the best memories. Piling onto the bus yet again was a snapshot moment of silliness forever captured in my mind. I would never have believed I could have that much fun riding a city bus, but the girl power aboard had it goin' on all over the place. Frannie's hilarious discourse with the bus driver alone was worth the ride. It was as if two long lost comic souls had reunited to perform a routine. The rest of us kibitzed with neighboring co-riders commuting to work, happily abandoning the concept of not talking to strangers.

The supreme best though came from Nancy's observant ways. I hadn't a clue that our vehicle was traveling in tandem, didn't even know they did such a thing with buses. I'll explain. Our bus was two in one, having both a front section with a driver, and a rear caboose area. Just as subway or train cars are connected one to another with some sort of accordion like gizmo, so too was this bus. Now here's where it got cool. Nancy observed the flooring joining the two halves together flexing and bowing as we took curves and corners. Jumping from her seat, she stood with one foot in either section and basically surfed the streets of

Chicago. Of course as soon as I heard her doing this, I was all over the wanting to do, and did. It was crazy fun as we laughed and whoa-ed along. I'm giving two major thumbs up to this means of transiting, and if you ever happen to be in Chicago, make sure to hang ten on the tandem bus.

The jonesing coffee hounds of our group would go no further until addiction was satiated, so a nearby breakfast diner was dived into as quickly as possible. Over eggs and pork products we relived Kim's morning glory and commenced to plotting and planning all we would do. Realizing we were only a hop, skip, and a jump away from one of Chicago's newest parks, we promptly threw down napkins, paid up, and toddled on over to Millennium Park.

Looking ahead to the dawning of a new millennium, Mayor Richard M. Daily and the great city of Chicago saw fit to commission the construction of a new park honoring the changing time. The twenty-five acre conversion of land from railways and parking lots took a little longer and more money than initially anticipated, but the job was finally complete only four years late and three times over its original budget with a final price tag of a mere 475 million dollars. What it lacked in financial planning was well made up for in the park's ability to attract the interested with its outdoor arenas, modern art structures, fountains, and lovely gardens. On July 16th, 2004, Millennium Park's opening was celebrated grandly with fanfare and festivities. Our being there exactly two years and a day later was not as celebrated, but was no less grand.

I knew little to nothing about Millennium Park prior to our visit, with one small exception, the fabled giant jelly bean residing in its midst. Being one of my favorite forms of candy, I knew I must meet it and see it for myself. Brilliant was the blue sky above as the hot summer sun glared down upon the earth. The sighting of a shining silver object became easily apparent and drew us to it like moths to a flame. The amazing stainless steel structure officially known as the Cloud Gate lay in wait before us. Although designed to represent a droplet of mercury, the locals have lovingly bestowed the nickname, the Bean, due to its familiar shape.

What little usable vision I have these days is still able to perceive light, but standing before the Bean's shiny mirrored surface reflecting the sun's unrelenting rays brought a whole new meaning to being blind. So bright was it that even with my diminished sight and sunglass protected eyes, I could barely keep my eyes open to look at the structure. The light overload was astounding and I believe could only be equated to standing directly in front of the sun itself. Along those same lines was the heat captured by the polished metal too intense to touch. I marveled at the immensity and felt the smooth curved surface from a far cooler vantage point, beneath and behind it. The three story Cloud Gate's reflection of sky and cityscape was dazzling to say the least.

If you ever find yourself in Chicago's Millennium Park, there are a few noteworthy sites I suggest you take in.

The Jay Pritzker Pavilion:

The philanthropic family Pritzker funded the creation of this musical pavilion and gave home to the Grant Park Music Festival, a series of free classical concerts. The band shell construct was imagined by world renowned architect Frank Gehry, and creatively designed to resemble the appearance of a blooming flower. Our brief visit to the pavilion consisted of us cutting through the area in search of shade. Neither pomp nor circumstance was called for on this hot summer day.

Lurie Garden:

The perfect incarnation of Chicago's motto "city in a garden" is this little stretch of foliage. The garden's beauty is reflective of its namesake, Ann Lurie, a generous humanitarian and hands on good deed doer. The two and a half acres consisting of flowers, trees, and lots of pretty things, is part of Millennium Park's green roof effort. Built on an existing parking garage roof top, the vegetative state has become the largest of this kind in the world.

The Exelon Pavilions:

I am completely a non-fan of corporate America claiming naming rights of anything, and typically will ignore a 'paid-for' title if possible. However, I'm making an exception to this rule for a moment to share the cool eco-friendly thing these four pavilions do. They are, like, totally solar powered, dude. Enough energy is generated to meet the electrical needs of a dozen Chicago homes. In addition, three of the pavilions lead to the underbelly of the park and the garage holding it all up, while the fourth serves as the welcome center. Several other attractions can be visited in Millennium Park, and can be learned about via this welcome process. But since I really want to move onto the fun portion of this tale, and since corporate names are plastered all over them, I'm just going to move on.

Hotter than a cat on a tin roof, or something like that, Chicago was well on its way to heating up to a mere 102 degrees. That'd be 110 with heat index don'cha know. Therefore, it seemed completely appropriate when the decision was made for some of us alleged adults to go play in the water fountain of this park. Mind you, Sarah was not among the gaggle of children leading the way, but she was all too willing to bring up the rear. I would normally ask for eyes to be closed as I guide one's mind into imagining, but this could prove to be most difficult, with reading and all. Instead, stay with me as I attempt to literally illustrate the unique Crown Fountain of Millennium Park.

It felt as though the city was slipping away with each step drawing me nearer to the majestic Crown Fountain. The sounds of water falling, along with the delighted giggles of small children, filled my ears and my heart with excitement. I had anticipated some sort of wall confining the fountains contents, and was initially confused when told I was at its edge, even though my stick detected no boundary. As understanding sifted into my mind, I comprehended the gentle sloping of the ground keeping the fountain's water at bay. Within the pooled liquid stood two monolithic towers, appearing to be made of blocks of glass. Water danced along the glistening walls as it cascaded from above down into the shallows below.

Peeking from behind the falling waters appeared grand projected faces of Chicago's multicultured inhabitants. One slipped into the next as they smiled down upon us, winked, and on the occasion, impishly stuck a tongue out. It was delightful and only made better when the waters flow was momentarily halted. Seconds passed and a face morphed to yet another, showing a puckering puss, and from those lips came the sudden spewing of water. Although the behavior of spitting is frowned upon by most, those present found great joy in its spray and would make a mad dash to be included.

Hopefully by now you have conjured up an image of the Crown Fountain based on my words. Let's side track a bit and talk irony for a second. That mental picture you have just created comes from this blind woman's description which was, wait for it, once described to me. Whoa, kinda mind boggling ain't it. I felt the need to make mention of this, wanting to emphasize a couple of points here. First, even with the best narration, the givers powers of observation, and the god given ability to paint a picture, it is completely up to the recipient's mind to get it going on. Undoubtedly each of you are all seeing in your mind's eye something quite different which brings me to my second point. This is why I'm all about the hands on experience to help clarify my vision. Without the ability to visually confirm an object, and taking the previously cited reasons into consideration, I adapt with my touchy feely ways. It also provides the excuse that permits me to get away with so very much. For purposes of clarification relevant to this particular encounter in Chicago, I felt compelled, obligated even, to get in touch, as it were, with the Crown Fountain my own self.

I stood at the fountain's edge with Nancy, who was the afore mentioned person describing things to me. The sun beat down, slowly melting me, and I began to feel taunted by the cool liquid just beyond my toes. Nancy, being on first name basis with her inner child, once again embraced the kid within, and the three of us happily headed into the Crown Fountain's wetness to play and explore. Entering the pool provided immediate relief and was a welcome escape from the increasing heat of the day.

Wading ankle deep over to the water plummeting from the tower's roof top, I stuck my hands in to feel the force of the fall. A nearly six story droplet drop picks up tremendous momentum in its descent, and when combined with millions of watery comrades, the pummeling becomes significant. Curious as to the breadth of the tower before us, descriptive words would no longer satisfy; I felt the urge to feel my way into comprehension. Laying hands on the glass block towers meant one thing, total submersion into the cascading falls. And so we did.

Taking the plunge were, of course me, Kim, Nancy, and, the true child in our midst, Sarah. A rousing game of follow the leader began our jaunt around the four cornered sides of the tower. We giggled and whooped as we slid along the slippery glass walls, enjoying the saturating sensation of the water pouring down over us. Once round, we squirted back out and stood soaked to the skin laughing. It's amazing how incredibly freeing playing is, and apparently rather entertaining too, for a number of spectators were just as amused by our antics as we were.

Water play not over with; we too had to be spit on by the fountain's faces. Timing was everything, and so was beating those toddlers to the out pouring spray. We danced with child-like glee, thoroughly uninhibited by age or care. It's the simplicities of life, daring to partake, and letting loose that often defines what is meaningful and memorable.

MORE THAN FUN AND GAMES

Sitting all splayed out, our soggy group thought it best to try and dry a bit before catching the bus back to our hotel. Low and behold, as our bodies baked, we were entertained by a juggling mime clown. Okay, the rest of them were entertained, not so much me since I'm generally not the target audience these silent types would go for. Not having much else to do for the moment, I simply took in the sun and stewed in my own juices. It wasn't long though before I began to feel a queasy unpleasantness in my belly. Taking into consideration our current locale and the means of getting back to a more inviting restroom, it dawned on me I better get moving before something else did first.

I shared my concern with Kim and made known the growing urgency. From the time it took us to re-apply footwear and walk to the bus stop, I knew my situation was becoming dire. Wooziness now accompanied my nauseated self, while my weakening legs forced me to sit. Waiting in the bus shelter seemed terminally long as my condition further deteriorated. My suggestion to screw the bus and catch a cab was quickly met with Jud B. all but throwing herself in front of the vehicle to get the driver's attention.

The befuddled cabby circled the city blocks confusedly until Jud B grew tired of his ignorance and provided him with much needed direction. Getting out of the car required more effort from me than my getting up this morning, but I managed to make it out and up to our room. And then, the exorcism began. All forms of vile, indescribable not niceties began pouring from any and all orifices of my body. I was my own worst horror movie. If I could have stopped for even a moment I would have told the others to get out while they still could.

Both Nancy and Frannie had separated from the fold back at Millennium Park. They wanted to take in some of Chicago's famous architecture in those parts. They had no way of knowing what was happening in the meantime, but soon learned when walking into the middle of my disintegration. I was laying in bed buried beneath a mountain of blankets freezing to death. Slipping in and out of wakefulness I caught pieces of the conversation taking place on my behalf. Phone call was made to the "Doctors Inn" service, which advised I be taken immediately to the emergency room. Summarily the decision to drive me there was dismissed due to the fact I was in no condition to walk, and nobody knew where to find a hospital anyway. 911 called, the ambulance arrived with a couple of strappin' EMT fellows. I mean that strappin' in the most literal sense since that's what they promptly did to me as they hoisted my weakened self onto the gurney and cinched me in. The mother in me still had the strength to delegate care though, and I placed Jud B in the good hands of Sarah, or maybe it was the other way round. Rolled out and Kim in tow, I was off to see about my well-being.

Seemingly rather sudden, I was thoroughly overcome with heat exhaustion and dehydration. Honestly, I thought I was drinking enough, but apparently I sweat more profusely than I care to admit or think about. Despite this disgusting turn of events, actually because of it, I can share my very own Chicago ER story.

I'll begin by saying; I am greatly impressed with the Lincoln Park emergency room and their staff. Friendly, efficient, and accepting are just some of the words I'd use to describe my visit. Never once was there a question about Kim being by my side, she was allowed in with me, of course after she filled out a dozen forms or so. Kim occupied with paperwork gave me the opportunity to chat up my nurse, which had me learning of her own gayness. The clue, telling me she and her partner were going to watch some friends participate in the ballroom dancing of the Gay Games. Remember I'm sick here; subtleties certainly weren't going to work on me. Despite my dried out, lethargic way of being, I still managed to crack my own self up with my wit—the nurse too. The IV already in, she had to change me into one of those adorable hospital frocks. As the nurse gently unclothed me, I couldn't help saying, "We've only just met, and already you have my shirt off." How fetching I must've been all fevered up and raisin dry.

Pumping in the missing fluids along with some anti-nausea medications, my discharge came quicker than I would have anticipated. I was still weakened and unable to stand on my own. To say I was cold in the middle of a summer heat wave cooking up three digit temperatures, seemed absurd but was true. It's how I got a swell hospital blanket for keeps since it cocooned me as I was wheel chaired out of the ER.

The little something they slipped me in my IV rendered me quite useless, and at times rather unconscious. When fleeting wakefulness occurred, my body had difficulty following my brain's commands, refusing to move without extraordinary effort. I have no clear recollection of the taxi ride home or much about being dumped at the hotel door. The drug induced fog cleared briefly, as I realized I'd have to somehow make it from the hotel lobby and up to the room. Kim had sought out assistance, and the cavalry arrived in the form of Sarah and Jud B. Their relief to know I was okay and back again quickly changed to the unspoken question of, "how the hell are we gonna move her?"

Their shoulders and my armpits provided the solution as they hoisted me up and braced me on either side. The ride up in the shoebox sized elevator was stifling hot, made worse by sharing it with another couple and their luggage. My fading lucidity nearly became disastrous as my legs buckled, but Jud B's shoulder redeployed under my rib cage, and kept me from finding the floor. Sheer determination and tremendous effort finally landed my sorry ass in bed.

The primary care instructions from the hospital advised the pushing of fluids. My overbearing caretaker's, Kim and Sarah, interpreted this as "drink, drink, drink!" A notion that may be all well and good, but it required some alertness from me to be completed. The how to and what to solution came in the forms of Kim and Sarah harassing me every few minutes into drinking a vile concoction of Gatorade. Vaguely I remember feeling irritated as it seemed they were always disturbing my slumber, yet compliance was insisted upon by Attila the nurse, formerly known as my baby girl Sarah.

Another hospital discharge order seemed on the obvious side, but probably needed saying for liability sake. Stay out of the heat. To accomplish this command meant keeping cooped up in the very well-conditioned air of the great inside. Butt kicking drugs, dehydration hangover, and humidity all led me to easy agreement, and I remained in our hotel room for the rest of the day and all the next. As I see it, I really got my monies worth out of our accommodations. Thing is though, we had planned on taking in a Cubs ballgame and, more importantly, some deep dish pizza along the way. As I rested, too tired to even pout or woe-is-me myself, I received the best phone call a girl can get. The gang who had went about their business of seeing a few sites, decided to skip the game and bring one of Chicago's world renowned za's directly to me. It was the best I ever had! Not so much from taste, my stomach really wasn't ready for it yet, but because of the grand gesture behind it.

This group of ladies I traveled with, they are the people you would want around in an emergency. Each stepped into their part as if pre-assigned, and took care of me until my butt was hauled away. The entire thing, and the manner in which I was being sick, could've been greatly humiliating, and yet it was not. I mean really, losing your lunch and shorts all at the same time is not exactly dignifying. My thanks go out to Jud B for valiant clean-up efforts, Nancy and Fran for contacting the house doc and arranging my departure, and to Sarah and Kim for getting back from unmentionable shopping in the nick of time. Even more, I'm thankful for Sarah and Jud B's willingness to hang out a bit during my ER-ing. I didn't have to worry about either of them while indisposed. Mostly I'm thankful to Kim for going above and beyond the call, and being there when I really needed her to be. Thank you all y'all for taking such good care of me!

WHILE I WAS SLEEPING

Discussions had and agreement made, we all knew we didn't have to do everything as a group during our travels. The interests of these individuals are as varied as the offerings of Chicago, so it seemed likely we'd go our separate ways at times. Little did I know that meant, when I was down, they'd all go out. What did I need'em hangin' around for anyway, to watch me sleep? Although I wasn't involved in any of the following, I thought I give a mention to what everyone else did. Ya know, kind of an after telling after they told me about it sort of thing.

Frannie and Nancy were on a walk scoping out Chicago's intriguing architecture. The big burn of 1871, also referred to as the Chicago Fire, led to a building boom and the resulting city rebirth. I know basically bupkis about this sort of thing, but did recognize the name of one famous contributor to the city's structural uprising, Frank Lloyd Wright. At least I did after I figured out he wasn't either of the flying Wright Brothers. His famous Prairie Style designs took homes in a whole new direction, and literally outside the boxed brand of building. Many guided tours exploring Chicago's famous constructs are available. Sometimes though, it's simply nice to take a stroll like the girls did.

Prior to my full blown dehydration destruction, Jud B. went on her own fact finding tour. Having only one site on her must see list, Jud B. slipped away to her golden Mecca of marvelous technology. A little empire best known as Apple had a nearby mega store, and our gal pal was all about an afternoon delight with the goods. In her glory and checking things out, she hung with homies a third her age as they messed around with the Garage Band program, teaching and learning from each other. The chance to do the computer gig was just the fix Jud B needed, and sent her mind whirring with new ideas for her docu-filming.

As I was whisked away by sirened ambulance, Sarah and Jud planned to stay together and occupy their time and minds with a walk to Navy Pier. Built in 1916, it originally was named Chicago Municipal Pier and served as a freighter dock. The pier's use became more popular as a gathering place for recreation and entertainment, until World War II, when it was once again transformed and became a training place for the U.S. Navy and bearer of its current name. After a period of disuse during the 60's and 70's, Navy Pier's resurrection came by way of the arts, entertainment, and shopping, making it one of the most popular places to visit in Chicago. Thing is; none of us did. Sarah and Jud B.'s heart wasn't much into frolicking thanks to the oppressive heat and a little bit of worry.

While fluids seeped back into my body via IV, the girls had places to be and people to see. Frannie had planned an outing with Nancy to catch a concert by her cello idol, David Finkle. It was a fair trade deal the two of them had worked out, completing the first half of the bargain a day earlier when Nancy opted to see a film about her own fella, Leonard Cohen. Traveling distances to the far outreaches of God knows where, the concert going gals had growing concerns about spending the night in the boonies as the music played on. Encore given, last note heard, the two of them all but hurdled the appreciating audience to get gone. Not since that inspirational star over Bethlehem, has a light source so compelled people into motion—until now. The girls approach on the station quickened when the light of the last oncoming train was glimpsed barreling down the track. As if on winged feet, or more likely winged prayer, the mad home stretch dash was made and finished line crossed when they entered the train. Their victorious prizes were utter relief and available seating, oh, and a trip home to bed.

The next morning was far more leisurely since we weren't running to catch another Kim race. Rising from bed when able and wanting, everyone did their own thing through the pre-noon hours. Sarah and Kim dipped in the hotel pool, I slept, and the rest of them disappeared somewhere. We convened again over lunch by the lovely pool side atrium. An earlier reconnaissance mission had turned up a local grocery store from which we purchased many items to make up our meals. I'm telling you, this is the only way to afford city eating. The business portion of our lunch was called to order and discussions had regarding the day's progression. The gals grappled with the polite way to tell me I best stay put, but nonexistent energy and the frequent need for a nap had me in full agreement. So off I went to bed again, while the gang went to loop the city.

If you really want to live like the natives and get a feel for the city, a body has got to ride the "L". The abbreviated nickname refers to Chicago's very own and much ridden elevated train system. Although commonly used for mass transit purposes, the gang adopted a more seeing sites approach to the ride. The Loop of the El encircles the downtown business district, landing commuters close to work. For those folks with a little more time on their hands, there are abundant offerings in the heart of the city. From viewing the spectacular skyline of Chicago, to the theaters, museums, restaurants, and the exquisite shopping of the Magnificent Mile on Michigan Avenue; a vacationer lacks for nothing to do.

Sections of the original 1892 tracks are still utilized today by the green line, and as interesting as that is, it's the additions making up the loop that make for good history telling. Back in the day the business district and its surrounding neighborhoods were rather persnickety about who and what was allowed in—the elevated trains being no exception. Due to a prohibitive law regarding construction, the only way to garner permission to build was by obtaining the written consent of property owners. Along comes this streetcar titan, Charles Tyson Yerkes, who uses his influential load of money to "convince" owners sitting on the west side of the proposed route into agreement. Needed signatures obtained, construction commenced, lifting the elevated tracks up and a tad over the east siders. Mr. Yerkes got his way, the last laugh even, and Chicago its "L" Loop.

Since I was sleeping when the gang rode the "L" rails, I ended up getting the low down later from Sarah. Astounded by the extreme close proximity of the train and its tracks to the buildings people lived in, Sarah soon learned of her voyeuristic tendencies as she tried to see inside the apartments. Catching glimpses of how Chicago dwellers live as she whizzed by at many miles per hour wasn't easy, but became a part of the challenge from this unexpected site seeing enjoyment. So if you folks on the "L" line are reading this, consider yourselves warned, and know it's more than the Peeping Toms of the world watching you.

THE RAT RACE

Getting up at 3:45AM twice in one week, while on vacation even, is going above and way beyond the call of dedication. I'm speaking of Kim's to the race, and our cheer team to Kim. Minus Sarah that is, for her allegiance had waned by this time, as she opted to stay nested in bed on this particular morning. It's really too bad though, because she missed a cool meet and greet with one of Chicago's very own wildlife inhabitants.

Somewhere along the way, it was realized the train was a far faster and more efficient means of travel than the bus, so our gang headed underground. A body never knows what it'll bump into at four something in the morning in a big city subway. There's the possibility of tourists, but I'm thinkin' not so much. Commuters, very likely. And then there are those creatures of the night—of the rat variety, not the blood sucking vampire or working lady kinds. And wouldn't you know it, that's exactly what we came across, a genuine, nocturnal, city rat in the subway.

There we were, we five with a few other weary eyed waiters. Frannie announced as she peered onto the tracks, "Hey, there's a rat down here." Her voice was licked with neither panic nor disgust; rather, it was filled with curiosity and fascination. Everyone else had been sitting quietly, eyes barely open, when suddenly and simultaneously they rose to their feet and walked right over to take a peek for themselves. Me, I didn't budge. A rat would've looked the same to me no matter where I was. But what I saw was enough to let me see everyone move in unison to the bright yellow warning strip indicating peril ahead. Rapt attention was given, stimulated conversation had, and strangers became familiar on-lookers of this filthy little beast while marveling at its rat antics.

This was quite a sight I conjured up in my mind's eye. All those people excitedly watching a rat as if it was some rare, exotic creature. Among the most fascinated was the one person I thought would be heading in the other direction when told a rat was nearby, Kim. There she was following along from a safe distance, as the rat did whatever a rat does skulking down the tracks. I am of course making an assumption with assigning this type of movement by a rat, which is based on stereotyped portrayals in the literary and film medias. For all I know, the rat could have been sauntering along the tracks as it minded its own business. It was, however, its very business which had Kim watching him most closely from a distance. The whole scene was a hoot in my head and probably one of my most favorite moments while in Chicago. What a rotten time Sarah picked to sleep in!

I don't know how Kim's 5K race could possibly top our rat watch experience, and I'm not completely sure I should compare the two. So maybe I won't. The only thing I'll say more about the one in regards to the other is, I don't think Kim had as much enthusiasm going into this race as she did in watching the rat. Maybe the thrill was gone after the first run. Maybe another early humid morning running didn't sound anywhere as good as sleeping in an air conditioned hotel room. Or, maybe the close encounter of a rat kind was just too stimulating. I don't know, I can only suppose. Better yet, I'll just move on now.

The Chicago sky was heavy with the haze of humidity and presented yet another morning for non-conducive running conditions. Tiredly Kim crossed the starting line and soon disappeared into the mass of competitors. Running the short race of a 5K, Kim could practically do it in her sleep, which is exactly how she approached this jaunt. I nearly mistook heavy breathing for snoring when I received Kim's customary call from the course as she updated us to her whereabouts. It confirmed what I already knew; the gal wanted the bed more than her sneakers this morning.

Our time our own for a bit as we waited, and shyness nonexistent among our merry band, we once again found someone to chat up. A young Aussie fellow had traveled half way around the world to be present for the GAY GAMES. Upon further inquisition, pardon me, I mean discussion; we learned he had signed up for the 5K. Unfortunately time zones and jet lag foiled his attempt to participate as he overslept and missed the start. Collective disbelief sent us into a kind of mothering, meddling, problem solving mode. Despite our words of encouragement and prodding him to do the race anyway, the rule following Aussie would not budge.

A different approach to the problem was needed, and didn't include leaving him alone. A proposed staging was suggested of a photo finish sort. Convincing the young Aussie to pop out onto the course and jog across the finish line as snapshots would be taken was something his conscience could live with. Off he went to conclude the fictitious race and photos were taken chronicling his every move. Upon review, he was not satisfied with his appearance and requested a re-do. Such the typical gay man, it's always about the look. Whether he fesses up the truth or not to his pals down under, we'll never know; either way he's got a mighty fine story about his time in Chicago.

ON ICE

As ever, time flies when having fun, and so it did with our final morning in the Windy City. Kim completed her 5K meandering in less than record breaking time; nonetheless, her participation was what counted. During the packing up process, the group decided to catch one last event before leaving Chicago and the Gay Games behind. The obvious choice became pair's figure skating, especially since tickets were purchased the day before. What wasn't realized until we arrived was, the morning hours were scheduled for practice, the actual competition would be later in the day. Unswayed by this fact, we agreed it would be worthwhile to observe the couples at work.

I grew up my whole life watching the Olympic pair's figure skating. Clean cut, wholesome couples, with a tall skinny guy hoisting and tossing about the minniest version of a woman. This indelible impression had to be somehow pushed aside in my brain. The blind thing was a challenge to over-come, even in my mind's eye, because I kept slipping back into known images. But with great effort I managed to create an accurate picture of the Gay Games pairs skate. The concept was same gender couples twisting and twirling on the ice. What I had trouble grasping was, how'd they decide who would be the "guy" and who's gonna do the girl part? With a re-think on gender roles and my trusty frozen companions filling me in, I began to see it more clearly.

The boys we observed practicing skated to a pumped up version of the music from Broke Back Mountain, keeping the cowboy theme with hats and all. Their couple style was a kind of side by side synchronized skating, like in ice dancing. The ladies' approach cleverly adopted a leaning into one another skating manner, and conveyed perfectly their music, Lean on Me. Gender specific roles were not assigned; rather it was more about being equals, complimenting one another, and mirroring movements. I was fascinated by the snippets of commentary I received, but even more, I noted in myself a proud feeling and excitement for these skater's accomplishments. Again I was moved by the purpose of the Gay Games. Think about it, the participation in an organized event openly celebrating individuals as they are embracing and cheering them no matter the level of skill. That's what I'm talking about. Now if we can get life to imitate art more, I think we could learn an awful lot here.

Clad in nothing but our summer garb, we huddled close together for warmth as we spectated in this giant meat locker of an arena. My heartfelt excitement soon began to shiver and freeze. The notion of sustaining frost bite merely a day after experiencing heat stroke was not a relished one by me, or my companions. Prying our frozen bottoms from the metal bench, we penguined our way out into the heat, and thawed in approximately four seconds. Hotel check out already completed, it was time for us to head home, but not before want and need were first addressed.

Sarah the supreme shopper had been on the prowl for a Chicago sweatshirt, and almost had one in her mitts. If it weren't for the kid being on the wrong side of a closed store window that is. Saddled up and heading out of the city, Sarah had resigned herself to the disappointment and released a controlled sad sigh. Hope now gone; destiny stepped in. For as we sat at a traffic light, Sarah gazed out the van window longingly and, SCREAMED! She scared the crap out of me. Somehow she had seen over my shoulder a store display of sweatshirts. I'm telling you, the kid has mad skills when it comes to shopping, and the keen sight to back it up. Red light not yet green, Sarah jumped from the van and dragged me along behind her and into the Robert Morrison college bookstore. I can't say I've ever heard of this school, but its bold lettering and inclusion of "Chicago" on a sky blue hoody became exactly what my youngster wanted.

Want cared for with the minor; it was the adult fixes we tended to next. What would a road trip be unless ice cream was in one hand and coffee in the other? An accident if you're the driver, but fortunately Frannie's self-control is phenomenal. The woman was well able to pace herself and have all of the above. I marvel at her restraint. I personally lack the java gene; however it's apparent the remaining grown-ups have theirs in good working order. Clichéd though it is, Starbucks was our final stop in the big city. Ice cream came along down the road a bit with frequented rest areas and a Dairy Queen practically every other exit. Whether buzzed on caffeine, sugar, or from hanging with good friends, the near six hour trip home flew by just as the rest of our time in Chicago did.

CHICAGO POST

Before I say my good-byes to Chicago, I need to share a little post trip story or two with y'all. Remember those tickets that slipped from Nancy's pocket on our way to the opening ceremony at Soldier Field? Well, a gentleman from California found them lying somewhere on the street. This fellow attempted to locate us, even going as far as trying to track us down via the ticket office. Our unknown friend decided to put the tickets to use and attend the ceremony himself. It wasn't until weeks later that we learned of all these goings on, from a letter Kim received in the mail. Included was the afore explanation and the good man's thoughts of just how providential this strange occurrence was. He too was in town to partake in the games festivities; however he wasn't planning on attending the opening. Because of this chance find, he did go, and he felt compelled to tell us how much he enjoyed the event and its inspiring effect it had upon him.

Kim and I were happy enough knowing the tickets fell into the right hands, but our surprising letter wasn't at its end yet for the good man from California also included a check for the full amount of all the tickets. This was something above and beyond the call of decency, and clearly demonstrates the beautiful flow of karma. The group had pulled resources to re-purchase tickets and support one another over the mishap, and now the money had been restored to us. We put it to a group vote and unanimously agreed a celebratory dinner was in order. It was yet another chance to be together, relive the fun, and give a cheer to the good man in tribute.

The other little detail I wanted to tell everyone about is this. It took me just shy of four years to pay off my emergency room visit. Those stinking bills started pouring in about three months after we got home. From a doctor I allegedly saw, to the ambulance ride, pathologists, and on to the hospital, everybody apparently had their mitts on me, and now stood with their hands out. My insurance coughed up some of the dough, but I figured the hundreds I still owed was gonna take some time, and time it took. At ten dollars a month, I slowly wheedled my debt down. It almost became a game for me and Kim when the statement arrived in the mail and Kim announced the remaining balance. We literally cheered the lessening amount until the final happy dance in March 2010. You know, I think I should gather up the Chicago gals and have a bill burning party.

MY KIND OF TOWN

Our trip didn't go exactly as expected; regardless I would have to say Chicago was fabulous. Kim's suggestion on that cold winters day to be a part of the Gay Games, led us to the unforgiving heat of Chicago's summer. More importantly, it gave us the wonderful opportunity to witness a welcoming attitude, experience an open acceptance, and participate in supportive unity. A definite do-over is called for though, because I want to sink my teeth into a deep dish pizza and revel in its deliciousness. I want to catch that ball game at Wrigley Field and loop the city on the "L". I want to hit Navy Pier and maybe even climb Sears Tower-by elevator of course. Most of all, I want to spend more time with my favorite gal pals and see what newness we can find.

SITES UNSEEN TIPS

GET IN TOUCH

If a site is unseen by you, it is completely and only your responsibility to take matters into your own hands and get in touch. Let me clarify. I'm all for the hands on approach to site seeing, obviously; since I am the one seeking to cop a feel. I should therefore be the one seeking the permission. It is my obligation to make the inquiry, and in no way should it fall to the guide. Not even under the "other duties as assigned" clause. If it's something you want to do, then you step up and ask.

Okay, you may have picked up a strong, tell you what to do tone in my words. That's because I was. The reason for my passionate belief of self-assertion is the too frequent occurrence of a person who should have been talking to me, talks to my guide instead. I know the deaf folks get this a lot too. Listen bub, I may not be able to see, but I sure can think, speak on my own behalf, and yes, even sign the slip of paper of the credit card I just handed you! Stand up for yourself, be assertive and ask away; what's it going to hurt? Your pride as a capable person to represent yourself if you don't. Oh, and who knows, you might even get the chance to touch something others can't.

ANOTHER TOUCHY FEELY WAY

We are blessed as humans to possess five wonderful senses to explore and experience our world, but it's the gift of appreciation which makes them truly spectacular. My waning vision has not bestowed upon me some super sense-ability to make up for the loss, instead it's my willingness to be aware and appreciate in a whole other way. It's the "use what I got" sort of thing, and try not to mope on what I don't.

Take for instance the awesome experience I had in Millennium Park's Crown Fountains. I conjured up my own image based on the descriptions given me, and then I took the plunge to get a hands-on feel for it. It wasn't just the fact that I was feeling the water all around me, the tower walls, and hearing the laughter of my friends and the children playing, it's so much more than that. Even my getting sick became a means to appreciate and be grateful. Don't get me wrong; I really wouldn't want to go through all that again thank you very much.

I don't want to be all preachy-like, I'd really rather encourage you by saying, look at life and all the wonderful opportunities. As for me, I have the best ability of all, the unadulterated capacity to appreciate, and with it, be grateful. Mind you, I'm no saint, or nothing like one. I'm a regular woman who just knows it feels better to have fun, count the blessings, and appreciate the hell out of things.

4

SAN FRANCISCO, CALIFORNIA

Summer vacation planning is always an interesting process. I'd like to say destinations are chosen by a burning need to go wherever, but financial realities are more likely the influencers of choice. Every so often though, both want and need align, and so it was with our decision to go to San Francisco. Kim and I always had this California spot on our travel bucket list, and when opportunity presented itself, we jumped all over it.

Our next trip decision was figuring out what method of convincing to get my mother to agree to come with us. You see, she resided on the right coast living north of Philadelphia. The haul to join us way on the other side of the country, traveling all by herself over multiple legged flights was no small request. Enticements given and proper amounts of guilt applied, she finally agreed to join us. The clincher being the ever growing up, rarely seen granddaughter, Sarah, who would be making the trip also. It was our Ohio home life, the eight hour car ride separating them that kept these particular generations apart, but a fun little trip across the country would fix that right up. Destination decided, participants picked, flights financed, we were all ready for a wonderful vacation together.

The city of San Francisco is a true blue example of an American city at its best. Famed landmarks have reached beyond its borders to inspire genres of film, television, music, and the written word. Its political and societal influences have led generations into seeking change and demanding it be carried out. Its neighborhoods and its peoples are as vast and varied as America itself and have also welcomed those many wanting a new start to life.

As our trip drew near, it seemed I repeatedly heard references to this city by the bay. Or maybe it was the song loop in my mind that kept playing, "If you're going to San Francisco, be sure to wear some flowers in your hair . . ." Not really a fan of the song, and quite sure I wasn't going to stick any posies into my short, unhippied locks, I was more than anxious to get this trip going.

HALF THE FUN

Somebody somewhere once said, "Getting there is half the fun." I not only disagree with this absurd notion, I must assert my protest in its utterance. Matter of fact, I suggest to those making such a ludicrous remark, one of two things seem obvious. Either the chosen destination really sucked, or they're just out of their ever lovin' mind.

Despite the many conveniences of modern day travel, I have always preferred the actual destination over the getting there process. Don't get me wrong, I appreciate the jet plane approach to the literal travel part of traveling, with its rapid flight ways and all. But it still had me up hours before the crack of dawn, schlepping my well stuffed but not exceeding the weight limit suitcase, and sitting mightily close to perfect strangers on a food deprived flight. As I see it, none of these things could, or would make getting there be fun, much less half of it. Like ends justifying the mean, I have taken on the belief system regarding this aspect of travel. It's necessary, usually tolerable, and ultimately leads to the place a body wants to be.

I apologize for my relatively negative bent on this topic, especially since our trip to San Francisco was smooth. Yet, Kim's condition upon landing was anything but satisfactory. The early hustle and bustle, over all excitement, and her obsessive need for full work out in the middle of the night, led to a nasty headache and a general state of unpleasantness. Kim's enthusiasm paled, along with her complexion, as we waited on luggage and mother to appear at the baggage claim. Both showed up

105

virtually in unison and we happily reunited with our arrivals. Hugging on Mom and toting the bags, we set about to secure a cab.

A few other contributing factors further reduced poor Kim to a puddle of goo. The first among them was the sheer up and downedness of the streets of San Francisco. Television and movies have cashed in on these so called hills to create death defying car chases; spectacularly emphasizing the vertical lift of a vehicle when flying 90 miles an hour on uneven pavement. Our own air born experience came by way of our zealous taxi driver. Possibly a dude with a need for speed, or just wanting a good tip, our careening cabbie put the petal to the metal and had us flying. That giddy up feeling when the stomach lifts well into the lung region had us giggling and whooping with excitement. Everyone that is, except poor Kim, whose color was finally returning, as a sickly shade of green.

Add on the elevatorless hotel we checked ourselves into, forcing a two flight drag and thump suitcase haul, and the scant amounts of food Kim had consumed this day, and her deterioration was complete. The woman was suffering and only one cure existed, FAB—food, aspirin, and a flat bed. Technically that may be three, but if administered at the same time, you get the idea. Kim's convalescence ensued, and my point has been made. Getting there is absolutely not the half of fun, but being there is quite the other story.

BY THE BAY

Poking around quietly in a darkened room with Kim convalescing didn't seem like much fun, so our little threesome of Mom, Sarah, and I decided to hit the streets. With vague idea of our whereabouts and map in hand, we set out on foot for the Frisco bay. I'd like to point out that taking the direct route may get a body where they want to be faster, but it doesn't always promote the chance for discovery. Some might see this as getting lost, whereas I much prefer my developed coping skill and reasoning with calling it opportunity found. A girls gotta do, or go insane from being steered wrongly so much.

Now you'd think our first bit of excitement while on walk about would have been one of the well-knowns of the city. Instead, it was a tree that captivated our attention. My mother has always had the proverbial green thumb and coming across unknown vegetation without closer inspection would never do. The odd tree appeared to be molting its bark and had littered scores of nut-like acorns at its base. The familiar fragrant aroma easily nosed as we investigated. Mom's fascination piqued, she inquired later and learned it was one of the many Eucalyptus trees growing hardily in the bay area. Doing what I always do, I stuffed a few of the pods into my pocket to be examined more closely at another time, regarding them as little exploratory treasures. Eagerly anticipating our next discovery, I was ready for more.

Venturing forward through whatever park we were in, we crested a hill and, those of us who could see; saw the radiant orange glow of the Golden Gate Bridge. We'll talk color later, but for now, know our excitement was big. My vision may have been vicarious, but my feelings were genuinely mine. Description provided, I pictured the distant bridge spanning the waters of the bay. I felt the sun's rays on my skin and painted its brilliance upon the blue cloudless sky. My mind's eye was uncluttered, only seeing a perfect vista of the famous bridge before me. Sarah and Mom's voice revealed their amazement, driving home the reality of where we stood. Gratitude lifted beyond my thoughts, encompassing the moment, and the three generations sharing it.

Following the path fate had meant for us, or simply the one we stumbled upon, we trailed along the bay's edge and descended to a small beach area. Sneakers rapidly thrown off, our tootsies took the happy plunge. Describing the waters as cold would certainly be a gross understatement for our unsuspecting feet recoiled in horror from the shocking frigidity. Even at the peak of summer the temperature hovers around fifty degrees. Braced for a second go at it, and determined to get in there, three sets of tens soldiered on, and in.

Toes thoroughly numbed and a tad blue, Mom, Sarah, and I opportuned by sitting on the nearby steps leading directly into the water. Soaking in both sun and the reality of being in San Francisco, we relaxed and observed our surroundings. Other scenes found attention with the bridge being out of view, the foremost being the maniacs swimming in the bay. Mom shared in disbelief the aqua-antics, making sure I understood this wasn't some leisurely frolic. Rather, the wet suited swimmers, wind surfers, and what-nots went at it full tilt.

An island in view gave us something to wonder, both in its appearance as well as its nature. Might this be the infamous Alcatraz? Not having a clue, our seated wanderings drifted over to the docky wharf protuberances down the way. Conjecturing continued as we supposed this to be Fisherman's Wharf. A plan to check it out was hatched, but we weren't quite finished with our sit. It was wonderful taking it all in. Feeling the cool bay breeze, hearing the water lap at the steps we sat upon, and enjoying our being together. As if to complete this moment, the ever timely, and somewhat lesser known fog of Frisco began its slow gentle crawl over the waters. The billowy mass blanketed and enveloped what lay in its path, hiding from us what we knew to be there. Curtain dropped, we decided to go have that look we figured on.

FISHERMAN'S WHARF

The English language is truly an intriguing form of communication, bordering on perplexing even. I set before you an example, which if done correctly, will not only demonstrate my meaning, but will also permit me a nice segue. Taking the words "dock" and "wharf", I have always thought of them as synonymously interchangeable objects. Admittedly I am the non-sailing sort, so I believed my comprehension may have been limited by this fact. In wanting to suspend my ignorance, I turned an open mind to the dictionary for clarification.

Definitions abounded from this source and that, providing numerous meanings based upon each word's intended use. It all remained unclear until I came across a notation at dictionary.com. "A dock is the water next to a wharf or pier and it is not a solid thing, a wharf is built along and parallel to the shore, while a pier runs out and away." Not even wanting to get mixed up with a pier's purpose, I steered clear and focused on my words of choice. Comprehension replaced my confusion. It was all good and satisfying. I should've stopped there, but no, I had to read the list of synonyms too. Curse me for my insatiable curiosity of the similarly meant. There it was, on each other's list—dock on wharf and vice versa.

What's a girl to do then? Ignore the learned approach of course, and turn to pop culture. Had Otis Redding sung about sittin' on the wharf of the bay, or the namers decided upon Fisherman's Dock instead, I'd be having this same internal conversation but in reverse. As promised though, I have illustrated my point of the complexities of the English language, and in the doing, have provided a path to discuss what our little group did next in San Francisco.

Trading in the calming waters for the bustle of Fisherman's Wharf, we moved on and met up with our resurrected Kim. I think the confinement, although necessary, was making her nuts. Lying in bed and knowing we were out there having fun surely impacted her speedy recovery, not to mention appearance. Kim managed the more direct route to the wharf district and suddenly stood before us perked up and ready to play.

Since the late 1800's, Fisherman's Wharf has always been the place for local fishing types to bring in and sell the catch of the day. The wharf may have changed over the years; both the physical location of it, as well as its primary purpose, but it has always been a spectacle to behold. Entering the district we were immediately swallowed up by the carnival-like atmosphere. It was all there; food, street performers, and tourist traps galore. Countless opportunities existed to separate the visitor from their money. Souvenir shops, Ripley's believe it or nots, Trusso's waxy ways, and even the homeless with hand's out.

Sarah had barely stepped onto the wharf when the ogling began. The teen-aged need to shop is a natural force, a type of survival instinct if you will. So compelled, she couldn't stop herself from leering longingly at the pleasures waiting in store. Magnetized, she was pulled in. Me too for that matter since I happened to be attached to her elbow at the time. There we were, surrounded by a sea of souvenirs and wares.

I would like to deny it, but it seems I cannot any longer. Sarah is just a victim of her parentage. Nature versus nurture, I know not which, but the kid has the buying bug and she got it from . . . her father. Alright, maybe a little from me too. I can justify it though, since my need is a form of adaptation. Yes, I said adaptation. By the procurement of items it enables me to tactilely identify where I've been or what I've done. It is my 3-D postcard and scrapbook all in one. For the record I stand by this argument of need, but will confess a probably already known fact. I want that stuff. I love little do-dads replicating my travels, showing off my accomplishments. Oh sure, I could just have a photo album, but nothing is as good as copping a feel of some place I've been. Need, want, by any other justification, it's still the same; I gotta have my souvenirs.

Enough of my confessional already. I was talking about Sarah. I don't know what her rationale is, but she too wants her goodies. Finding a plethora of sweatshirts, jackets, and garments for wear, we perused this store front to back. I had heard that the #1 touristy item sold in San Francisco is what we were now looking at. Too frequently people underestimate the chill of this California destination and come unprepared to bundle. We were ready though thanks to extensive touristy research, yet unwilling to pass up such deals. Luxurious reversible embroidered jackets for $20. Polo shirts for $6. C'mon, zippered fleece sweatshirts only $12. It was a glorious shopping extravaganza, and one a teenage budget could afford.

The Fisherman's Wharf area went on for blocks and completely catered to the visiting tourist. The idea of taking in more seemed impossible, for our weary bodies had traveled far this day between flight and foot. Knowing the trek to the hotel would take some doing, we bolstered ourselves with the most perfect of foods, ice cream. Umph returned and readied for the walk, we set out to set out. That is, until we came across a most magnificent mecca of musical marvels. A store filled to its brim with beautiful and extraordinary instruments from around the globe.

Kim was in her glory as she thumped and plucked her way through the store's offerings. Ever the one to make music out of any available surface, the drums before her were more than a dream to play. Leaving Kim to bask in the bang, Sarah and I explored further. Stringed, chiming, airy, percussion pieces, so many wondrous representatives of musical instrumentation. Shaking, rattling, and rolling our way through, Sarah came across and was intrigued by a small wood carving of an owl. Despite our thorough inspection, we couldn't come up with a clue of what the thing was. I have instilled and always encouraged Sarah with the notion, "if in doubt, check it out," which has led to many inquiries over the years. Asking the store owner the owl's purpose, he demonstrated his answer by placing it to his lips and gave it a soft breathy blow. From the hollow carving came the distinct sound of an owl hoot. Pleasantly surprised by the likeness and the ease of its creation, we decided it had to be our musical trophy from this trip.

The day was all but complete. Energy and money both spent, we had only the trudge back to the hotel left. I can't prove this by any scientific means, but I know for a fact the hills of San Francisco grow larger after dark. Somehow with each step the incline increases. Like being on a sort of demonic carousal, the uphill walk made to the Fisherman's Wharf area turned and became even more up hellish returning. Unfathomable I know, but true nonetheless.

Praying for mercies, and cursing each unanswered step taken, we continued our climb into eventual bed. Fate not done with us yet, we quite accidentally crossed paths with Ghirardelli Square. The famous chocolate factory taunted its decadence before our eyes, noses, and mouths. Believe me or not, but know this truth, I didn't have nothin'—at least on this particular visit. The earlier ice cream had already satisfied my sweet tooth, but it didn't stop the others. Samples were nibbled and slobbered on, eliciting sounds of yummy satisfaction. Between chocolate buzzing and the elevated altitude, a true San Franciscan high concluded our night.

BUS STOP

Kim and I have visited a number of major American cities all in the name of site seeing. The plan to use the hop on and off bus tour has always been a positive experience for us. Maybe we're just lucky, or possibly have become expert at discerning a competent tour company. The reason for our success is most likely because there are many capable tours that exist out there. Whatever may be the cause, the effect of us having fun, learning a thing or two, and getting about has always been one of the easy parts when it comes to our trips.

As with any bus ride, it eventually comes to a stop. If only the ability to turn hindsight around existed, it would make decisions a bit easier to make. However, the little telltale signs shadowing the events to come inevitably become evident well after they occur. So it goes with life and in this very case, our tour bus experience in San Francisco.

Trudging over hills only, for nary a dale exists in this cardio stimulating city, we eventually located the tour bus ticket office in Fisherman's Wharf. Our passes procured, we climbed aboard and to the top of the awaiting double Decker open roofed vehicle. The tightly fitting packed to extreme capacity bus provided limited seating options, forcing us to squish our four selves into a three self spot. The first invisible precursor appeared and scampered right on by with each of the following signs we missed.

The bus sat completely unmoving. Passengers were sweating from the claustrophobically close conditions. The hapless group sat captive as the sun blazed down cooking them. I soon became aware of the listless murmurs of discontentment echoing all around me. The sighed breaths of hope were released. As it so often does, curiosity got the best of me, encouraging a little Q&A of my neighbor. Well, not so much neighbor as guy whose lap I was trying to avoid sitting on since we were mightily tight in the accommodation area. All too willing to voice his complaint, I soon learned these poor numb butted souls had been sitting for at least an hour already.

Almost as if in response to his statement, the bus engines rumbled to a start, lumbering it slowly forward. The movement provided the much needed return of hope, not to mention a slight breeziness as our behemoth of a vehicle crawled along. Anticipation briefly replaced awareness, until reality brought it back again. We had circled the same stupid block at least three times.

No announcements of explanations were given, not a single direction provided, only laps around the friggin' block with a load of perplexed passengers. As suddenly as we started, we stopped. I heard noises from below, faint sounds of someone saying, "Test test. Is this thing on?" Next thing we knew, a very caffeinated, or simply self perked, little Asian tour guide appeared with bullhorn in hand. Word spread quickly among the irritated that our bubbly guide overslept, and the PA system was taking the day off altogether.

Foreboding shadows hovered transparently over us as once again we moved. The bus lurched and swayed as it rumbled noisily along. Bubbles stood up front with her trusty bullhorn. We in the back packed like deaf sardines were unable to hear a single word she said. Between the bus and city sounds, and the lower tree branches attempting to take our heads clean off, it was absolutely impossible to hear. We, the poor unfortunate schmoes in the back of the bus, attempted to convey this point with a series of shouts and gestures to our boisterously blathering Bubbles. Maybe Bubbles just thought we were excitedly reacting to her tour, or maybe she thought we needed to stretch a bit. Whatever she interpreted, our meaning took some time to sink in, because it was a good while before the clue made contact. Bubbles bounded back to us and said with bullhorn blaring, "Why didn't you tell me sooner you couldn't hear?" And it was right there when hope's death collided with hindsight.

Escape by way of a hop-off point was not readily available, forcing us to endure Bubbles and her bullhorn. The woman was a menace, turning on us to blast incomprehensible words in our direction. Indifference was our only means of tolerance. At some point she wandered away a bit and my thoughts and Sarah's stomach turned its attention to finding food. Unfortunately, this was also about the time when insult was added to misery. A convertible bus might have had its advantages for site-seeing, but its lacking overhead protection gives way to open air mishaps. An overhead bird targeted poor Sarah, and delivered its payload. Pooh shrapnel flew with Mom sustaining a hit to her shoulder. The casualties were cleaned up as best as pocket Kleenex allowed. The effects were costly though, the long term damage to teenage psyche irreparable. We had to get off this hellish bus, and thankfully, our saving stop was the square right around the corner.

UNION SQUARE

A city, town, and even a burg would not be complete unless it has some sort of appointed place for its citizens to gather. Designs may be as varied as the small town park and obligatory gazebo, to the fountained stone surfaced setting of a larger metropolitan, but the purpose typically remains the same. These public squares, parks, gathering points allow people to come together in times of celebration, in memory of, or to make a statement. Such was the case for San Francisco's creation of Union Square. So named because of its initial use by the passionate citizens demonstrating their support for the Union as the American Civil War began to brew.

Seeing that I and my traveling cohorts were atop a tour bus while entering Union Square, one might think I learned that little naming fact there. Lord knows, it didn't happen that way at all. Instead we sought safe haven from this bus beast, and found it with an illustrious piece of real estate. Although desperate to hop off as rapidly as possible, we optioned to use the bus stairs rather than leaping over the open side. A short burst of relief washed over all of us as we gained our freedom, until other needs became evident and far more pressing. Food, a thorough hand washing, and a toilet, not necessarily in that order, appeared next on our agenda.

Today's Union Square is known for its high dollar shopping opportunities. A fact quickly made clear by the Neman Marcus looming right in front of us. Elite, chic, and out of our league, we decided what better place to use the facilities. In we went, and I was immediately overwhelmed with fear. The very air smelled rich. I could feel the hoity-toity all around me. My body instinctively responded by clenching up tight. Drawing normally loose appendages in, my stick near to me, and even my buttocks close, I walked carefully through the store. Maybe Sarah didn't grasp the swanky status here as she darted into the Prada boutique and handled $1500 purses, or maybe she didn't care. But I did and firmly told her to stop touching everything.

Now I've been using indoor plumbing for years, but nothing has ever prepared me for this department store toileting experience. Upon entering, it was as if stepping into someone's apartment. Mood set with soft lighting, the couched room was further accented with flowers, wall paintings, and a lovely area rug. Beyond this were individual powder rooms. I'm not talking just stalls, but actual separated, closed off by its own door, complete bathrooms with all the necessities and then some. Even around the mirror were those special make-up lights for face fixing. The piece de resistance though, was the exquisite paper products availed. Ooh dog, talk about the lap of luxury. So taken with our new accommodations, our haggard middle-classed selves sat a spell to enjoy our surroundings.

I'd like to say we moved on because we were ready to, but I think the more likely reason was when that fancy dressed woman came waltzing in. I don't know who was more surprised by our splayed out presence. We kind of pulled it together though, and got going shortly after her visit. We had to anyway, because Sarah's grumbellies needed tendin' to big time. The emersion from fancy fantasy and back into the real world let loose the grip on my body and led to the group discussion regarding lunch.

Between being hungry, bus disaster, bird ploppage, and decision making falling just short of a summit, Sarah's patience was low, non-existent to be more accurate. The kid needed food and a decision quickly, and God love them, Kim and Mom weren't exactly the spontaneously decisive ones in our group. I'd categorize them more like mullers. I barely uttered the words to Sarah, "Why don't you ask somebody . . .", when she was already accosting a local. Inquiry made and fast food burgers on our radar, Sarah and I just started walking. No exchanged words optioning ways to get there, just decisive movement. I heard Mom saying, "Are we going . . . ?" Then a slight pause as she noticed our leaving, and finished with, "I guess we are."

Taking charge and with food eminent, Sarah and I laughed as the other two straggled behind. Sarah's mood lightened with the knowledge of food on the horizon, and she began reading the various store names we were passing. My ears piqued with interest when she mentioned something somewhat recognizable-something sounding sort of like Bowden's. My brain began to whir with recognition, the remembrance that this very place is where it all started, the world famous sour dough bowls filled with clam chowder. Knowing the two behind us, knowing they wouldn't want burgers, knowing they would want something uniquely San Franciscan, I quickly turned to Sarah and got her permission to alter our plan and dine here.

Sourdough was discovered by Mr. Boudin when he replaced a common ingredient in the dough he was using to make his bread. I'd gladly tell you what it is, but I haven't a clue as to what goes into normal bread, much less this stuff. Nonetheless, I am quite adept at ordering what I like. Sandwiches and soups acquired we dug in to the yummies before us. For the record, soup, whether it's the clam chowder Kim chose, or the lovely cream of squash Mom got, is a brilliant culinary move. It is delicious, hearty, and eco-friendly with edible clean-up. Kudos to Mr. Boudin for his great discovery. I'd like to suggest the Nobel Prize be given for food, if it isn't already.

Hyde transformed back into Jekyll, Sarah was ready to explore again and off we went to the center of Union Square. This large one block area is frequented by downtown workers for lunch get-aways, tourists, and shoppers seeking a brief respite from the hunt. On our particular day of visit we had the good fortune to hear fun, bluesy music, with touches of country rock and jazz. The sound and the sun kept me company while the others went to do their shopping things. On a regular basis, Union Square plays host to a variety of free events, including but not limited to concerts, art exhibits, and food fests.

Bolstered by good food, music, and the joy of being in this awesome city, we felt ready to face the bus again. Heeding the unwritten rule of timing is everything; Sarah was dispatched to stand watch for the bus turning the corner onto Union Square. Signal given, we made way to the designated pick up point as the bus circled the square. Perfectly synchronized, we arrived at the stop and watched its approach. The big red double Decker hop on and off bus came, and, went. The thing just blew by us. Never once touching the brakes it kept on going, zooming right on by. If ever there was a proverbial final straw that surely was it. I put to vote we nix the bugger, catch a cable car back to Fisherman's

Wharf, and get our money back. Indignation raised, along with our dander, we unanimously agreed.

SAN FRANCISCO'S REAL TREAT

How many of you remember this happy little jingle? "Rice A Roni, the San Francisco treat . . . DING DING!" The advertisement stuck, but the rice never did. This was undoubtedly a pop classic commercial proclaiming both a city and quick rice in a 30 second spot. From this decades old ad millions associate cable cars and this wonderful city with boxed rice. I'm guilty as well, because as I stood in line to board this famed ride, I suddenly became aware of my singing the tune. And its mission accomplished for the great American advertisers, we've all been corrupted.

Nothing against the rice, but really I'm thinking the true San Francisco treat are the wonderful clanging cable cars. Necessity being the innovator of invention, these vehicles were created to haul cargo up the steep inclines of the San Fran streets. The previous method of horse drawn wagons had been extremely treacherous. The architect of the cable car, Andrew Hallidie, had witnessed the tragic accident of a horse slipping on the wet pavement and the gruesome carnage that resulted. Utterly horrified, he was determined to develop a much safer method of movement. God bless Mr. Hallidie, for his humanitarian efforts, engineering genius, and the thrilling ride we were about to have.

Just a couple of blocks from Union Square was one of the beginning-ending points for us to catch a cable car. The Powell-Hyde line runs from Hallidie Plaza to Fisherman's Wharf and was our obvious solution to our two pronged need. The first was, the return to the wharf for retribution; and the other, wanting to go for a ride! Taking on the mystique of more than merely a form of public transit, the cable cars have become synonymous with the city's allure and a must ride for tourists. The nominal cost and half hour wait in line was a fair price to pay for the chance to ride this interactive piece of history.

Those who could, watched with rapt fascination as each car entered the turn around, and were captivated by the simplicity in which they were handled. The cars themselves have no source of power or motorization. To be propelled forward, the driver moves a pincher-like device down into the groove in the street where the cable runs under the road, and grabs on. The best way for me to "grasp" its working is to think of the tow rope used to move skiers up a hill. The concept is the same, hold on when you want to move, let go when you want to stop. The conductor on board drives the thing, and it is he who has to know about braking, momentum, inertia, and all the technical stuff to keep passenger and machine safe and working.

The next piece of apparent easy ingenuity lay before us. When the Powell-Hyde line reaches its end, it moves onto a giant lazy Susan of sorts, and is literally turned around by two men. A complete about face brings the car to its beginning spot and ready to roll. Effortless in its appearance, my partners in description effused amazement and excitement as they relayed the goings-on before us.

I listened to the enthusiastic words provided me to paint the cable car scene on my mind's eye canvas. All the while curiosity attempted its distraction. The noise of constant clicking came from below the street surface, sounding as if hordes of crabs were clapping their claws. I was entranced with interest. Here is where the underground cables came to a kind of end, flowed across a system of pulleys and gears, and wound their way through until heading back again from where it came. The cable line is a closed loop, therefore ever circular in its journey.

Patience is never easier when captivated by your surroundings. Seemingly the minutes were but seconds, and our party had made it to the front of the boarding line. Devising a clever plan to assure us of an outside viewing seat, I moved Kim and Sarah into the first on position. Providing the young and abled with explicit instruction, I directed them to dash behind the cable car and get to the far side first. Their mission, jump on and sprawl out ensuring us all the primo seats. I then assigned Mom the duty of guiding me as I walked wide. Let me explain. I planned to tippy tap as wide a path as possible, in an attempt to hold back the masses behind us. I was, if you'll allow, the dam, or the dike as it were, to hold back the crowded tide.

Phase one was successfully carried out with Kim and Sarah doing their job. Phase three was working as I took advantage of the perks of blindness and people's natural fear of big sticks. It was phase two that I should've reviewed a little more closely, and gone over the rules of guidance with Mom. Oh sure, we got around the back of the car without incident, and even came up alongside to enter minus any problems. It was the part involving boarding, steps, and proper guidatory technique that led to a failure in communication. I vaguely remember being told, "There's steps'. Mind you, you must know I hadn't seen a cable car since I don't know when. And when I did see one, regrettably I didn't commit it to memory. Additionally, the toy replica of a cable car I had already purchased was not identical to the car we were about to ride. And lest you have forgotten, I'm blind. All these factors combined and led to what came next.

Sarah and Kim sat dutifully saving seats. Mom warned of the steps leading up to those seats. I tipped and tapped, reached out, and, SMACK! My forehead had connected with a very sturdy pole. Clanging bells rang inside my noggin as stars danced around it. Typically this pole is used for riders to hang on to, but in my case, its purpose changed to that of knocking blind women silly. Mom commenced to check my condition while profusely apologizing. Sarah laughed hysterically and provided no aid or usefulness whatsoever. And Kim, I think she was taking pictures of something like usual. Although senseless I remained determined to not lose my seat, and more carefully this time, I got aboard.

I'll never know if anyone saw my noodle knockin' moment, and to be honest I don't really care. These kinds of potential embarrassments have long since passed me by. I do believe however that karma sat nearby spectating. You see, using the perks of blindness for good is okay with the universe, but if it's just a plotted plan to manipulate others for some good seats, well, sometimes your bells gonna get rung to keep things in perspective. As for my kid laughing at my expense, she'll get hers someday. I know I did-thanks karma.

I was all about living the experience and ready to ride the cable car rails. I've seen the images back in the day of sight, the beautiful woman leaning out as her lover leaps to join her, all set with a scenic backdrop. So when more passengers squeezed on and filled the car to capacity, my romantic notions were pushed off and replaced with the utility purpose of a transport vehicle. I tell you, it was as starry eyed as being on a big city bus during rush hour.

Even if I were able to view a site, I wouldn't have seen a thing. Our seated selves were walled in by those standing passengers. Depending on your vantage point, crotches, guts, and boobs would've been the take home memory of the cable car ride. Fortunately though, as we progressed, some of those stand ups got off, and left us with room to spare. The circumstances finally availed; I was going to do the fabled cable dangle. Picture it, me hanging on, wistfully looking ahead as I soared up and down hills, enjoying the breeze through my hair. It was going to be grand.

What they don't show in those movies or famed commercials, is the cluttered condition of the street. If I had dangled as I wished, I would've been knocked clean off the cable car by a passing vehicle. Narrow streets and loads of traffic may have diminished the experience for others but not me. Imagination fully at work, I dared to dangle a bit and create the idea I was going for. The breeze did blow through my short hair and I felt the roll of the hills below. It was awesome, even with the restrictions placed upon me by a fearful daughter and mother. I truly had a blast. What a joy it was to be in San Francisco riding a cable car, and loving every conscious minute of it.

COMPLIMENTS OF THE BUS

I have little to no complimentary things to say about our experience on the hop on and off bus tour we attempted; that should be evident by now. I do recognize this may have been an isolated incident, at least the first part with delays and not hearing Bubbles. The blow by though, I later learned was not, and these matters needed straightening out.

Still joyful from flying over the streets of the city upon a cable car, I had to de-cable and began to prepare myself for the Refund War. Remember, the point of returning to Fisherman's Wharf was to settle the score with the bus company. Once again at the doors of the ticket office I naively entered earlier, I now knowingly suggested to Mom and Sarah, "wait outside." The innocent needn't witness the battle being waged on their behalf. Loins girded and game face on; I quickly whispered a reminder to Kim about not letting me run into anything. Passing through the doors and standing as tall as my full height would stretch, I politely confronted the same woman who had sold me the tickets earlier this morning.

I was ready for her. I had stories recounting the disaster we had embarked on. I was ready to use the big guns, whatever they were. Without warning she blurted out, "I'm sorry." Right up front, no questions asked. But I provided the answers anyway, because I was ready. She apologized and agreed to refund the money we had spent. Then, you know what she did next? That real friendly lady, she went and offered us four complimentary tickets on board a bay cruise. For nothing even.

What happened here? The nice lady threw me. I know, she must've heard tell of my lawyer-like skills in presenting evidence to support my case. My abilities to stand firm and not sway to corporate greed. My stick-wielding sense of justice. I had her at "hello". Yeah, that's it. She was no match for me, and she knew it. Pardon me as I synch up my bra straps and bravado about a bit. I am woman; hear me roar!

I took this peace offering to the group. Sarah only had to hear the cruise was passing under the Golden Gate Bridge, and she was all over the idea of going. Wrong righted, our happy little foursome agreed and was off to take an unexpected boat excursion.

CRUISING THE BAY

The San Francisco Bay is a large inlet of water and a microcosm of weather. Waters frigid, it typically only rises into the 50s on a good day. This bay remained hidden from Caucasian eyes for centuries thanks to surrounding mountains and rolling fog. Today, the bay is alive with activity from swimming and frolicking, to shipping cargo and tourists.

The perks of blindness came in handy for those in our group who needed to see the sites, by pre-boarding our boat and giving us choice seats for their viewing pleasure. For the record, this is completely a different and quite permissible use of the perks, in that I did not plot to obtain the good seats. I was offered the opportunity to board first, and therefore no karmic consequences were sustained. I'll be honest, since my view was unchanging no matter where I sat; I wasn't really looking forward to doing this bay cruise. Distant cityscapes are lost to my touchy feely ways. Not to mention, I've been on plenty of these kinds of boat rides before, and unless the thing is being tossed about on mighty waves, I usually get bored.

Thinking I had about an hour of nothingness to kill, I reluctantly placed the provided headset dutifully on my ears and tuned in the radio sitting on my lap. What came next was the total pleasant surprise of the wonderful narration on this tour. I want to give a shout out to the person who realized this means of broadcasting is far more effective than a public address system, or bull horn for that matter. Not only could I hear every word spoken, but I was wonderfully entertained with the tales associated with the sites unseen by me.

Shortly after leaving the dock, Sarah and Kim disappeared to snap photos. My ever loyal mother remained at my side filling in with color commentary, at least until she realized I was already deeply engrossed and missed half of what she was saying. Each of us in our own way took in the beautiful scenes San Francisco had to offer enjoying the so-called side tracks.

Coit Tower:

Easily noticed on the cruise, this landmark appeared to be fashioned in the shape of a fire hose nozzle. This alleged request has been attributed to the tower's benefactor Lillie Hitchcock Coit, who was the SF fire department's number one fan back in the day. Particularly fond of hanging with the boys of Knickerbockers Engine #5, Lilly was anything but typical. Uncustomary for the times, she wore pants, played poker, smoked cigars, and on the occasion, she chased fires with the fellas. Although this history may be slightly colorized, the tower's twenty-six murals are completely so. Expansive and sometimes controversial, the artwork has been restored and preserved for public viewing. Mrs. Coit's hope to beautify San Francisco has been well achieved.

Natural Inhabitants:

Oh those silly, lovable critters, the sea lions. Just as much an attraction as anything man-made, these indigenous dudes have claimed the docks of the bay as their very own. Unfortunately for us and our July visit, we scantly caught a glimpse of them, only learning later of the prime time appearance in the winter months. The noisy lot of them had gone south to mate, leaving only a few confirmed bachelors behind. When the whole gang returns in January, it's undoubtedly a rip roaring good time. Imagine hundreds of barking blubber laden denizens carousing and looking for that special someone to call their own.

The Golden Gate Bridge:

The unique vantage point of passing beneath it had Sarah all excited and snapping away with her camera. The immensity of the construct was more fully understood as it loomed mightily above us. An interesting little tidbit I picked up from the tour narration was about its color. Not even close to being golden, instead its vibrant color choice is that of International Orange, and difficult to work into a song. For example, "Open up your International Orange gates . . . ," doesn't quite have the same ring. The bridge painting is a never ending production, for as the crew completes the one side, it's time to head back again and slap another new coat on the other side.

Angel Island:

The largest of the bay islands, its occupation and use has varied greatly over the past hundreds of years. The Miwok Indians peacefully co-existed with nature upon the land. The Spaniard explorer, Ayala, was the first European of record to discover the island. Following the tradition of naming findings after the closest Catholic religious feast days, he declared it to be "Isla de Los Angeles", Spanish for island of the angels. Its use further adapted to an immigration station in the mid 1800's. Supposedly the "Ellis Island of the West", The U.S. government's attempt to limit the influx of Chinese had the immigration service referring to the site as "The Guardian of the Western Gate." Some Chinese were detained up to three years in quarantine or other detention type facilities until verification of their lineage to an American citizen could be proven. During World War II the structures were converted to a POW processing center for captured German and Japanese soldiers. Today Angel Island is a part of the National Park System. Its historic buildings are preserved for educational purposes and its land used for far more pleasurable activities like camping, hiking, and the enjoyment of the great outdoors.

Alcatraz Island:

Named "Alcatraces" by the Spaniards, its modern day derivation has been the result of white folks getting it wrong over the years. The original meaning translates loosely to "strange birds," an accurate description of those territorial bay gulls nesting there. With the onset of the Gold Rush, along with the booming population and money sitting in San Francisco, the U.S. Military thought it best to establish a strong protective presence. As the years progressed, the fortress' role shifted from keeping unwanteds out, to keeping them in. A military prison was established and began Alcatraz's long illustrious history of incarceration.

ROLL WITH IT

Sometimes, plans don't exactly go as planned. This is when a body has got to learn to roll with it, hang loose, go with the flow and simply make the necessary adjustments to get along. Of course a number of factors may enter in to determine the ease in which this is accomplished and the eventual outcome. Such things to consider are the people involved, the ability to make decisions, the level of frustration being experienced at the time, if anyone might be hungry again, etcetera, etcetera, etcetera. All are valid pieces of the altered plans puzzle, and most certainly a part of the traveling process. Conceptually I get this. It's the putting it into practice where I typically stumble. But on the occasion, the moon, stars, and my patience align, and the results lead to unknown adventures and moments of delight.

Rolling into our morning, we readied ourselves and hit the ground running with destinations in mind. A splendid ride on the cable car not only tickled our fancy, but also our curiosity as to its history and workings. A jaunt to its museum was in order. Furthering our excellent plan, we decided the conveniently nearby Chinatown should be included as a must see opportunity. The good folks of BART, the Bay Area Rapid Transit, just so happen to have a link going our way. How could it get any better I ask, and yet it did. Thanks to Sarah's keen sight and ability to read, she noted posted signs on the bus informing of fare reductions for seniors, the disabled, youths, and personal care attendants. Kim was designated as the latter, Mom, Sarah, and I got the rest, and we rode for practically nothing.

The plan was well executed with the bus delivering us near the cable car museum and the upwardly angled street to get there. Intent on the climb, we passed by the front doors initially and had to back track a smidge, laughing at ourselves as we did. Upon entering we soon realized this was a working museum, in that the actual motors, gears, and whozen-whatzies we were looking at enabled the cable cars to run. It was a rather noisy spot, especially noticed as my counterparts attempted to read pieces of information to me. At least it was until suddenly darkness and silence befell us simultaneously. Everything stopped moving, from coils winding through pulleys, to the people looking at them.

Although some consideration was given to what was happening, it wasn't enough to make us truly concerned. The windows provided light to read by, and finally able to hear, we agreed to keep browsing. Mom was reading this sign and that posted all about and ended up introducing me to Friedel Klussmann, better known as the Cable Car Lady. It was because of Ms. Klussmann's dogged determination and ability to motivate that we even have the cable cars today.

Back in the 1940's, The mayor of San Francisco deemed the cabled system to be out dated and wanted to rip this institution from the streets. Friedel would have none of it, wanting her beloved cars to remain intact and in use, so she began her plotting amidst a flower and arts convention. Apparently this is just the sort of place to start a revolution of this sort. Forming the Citizens Committee to Save the Cable Cars, Ms. Klussman gathered signatures to put it onto the ballot and in an overwhelming landslide of affirmation, 77% of San Francisco's voters agreed the cars should remain. The unyielding Cable Car Lady continued to champion the cause the rest of her life and at her passing at the age of ninety, the cars were draped in black in her honor. Today the Powell-Hyde turn-around, where we all waited to board and I began my love affair of the cable cars, is dedicated to this magnificent woman.

Having the dedicated plaque read aloud to me, and learning of Friedel Klussmann's triumphant role in the history of the cable car, I was moved to give her a "Rock on sista friend" shout out, doing so just prior to a museum employee's polite request for us to leave. Honest, it wasn't me getting us thrown out, rather it was the power outage and the need for safety that had everyone exiting the building. Upon departure, we learned the entire surrounding neighborhood was without electricity. Not only was a shadow cast over the neighborhood, but it lingered heavily over our plans.

To roll with it we had to banter about some ideas, and did until settling on one. Our motley crew decided to finish scaling the steep street we were standing on. Schlepping to the top of Nob Hill, we garnered incentive from the Painted Ladies residing there. Now before you go thinking things you shouldn't, I'll clarify and let you know that the colorful broads I speak of our brilliantly made up Victorian homes. Aesthetically fun and artsy, these homes have drawn tourists from far and wide, and have made appearances in photo books, movies, and even as the opening shot of the 80's sitcom Full House.

Street peak crested, we stood about catching our breaths and wondering where they were. I can't explain my thought process at the time, but for some silly reason I believed the houses would be nicely sitting there, waiting for us, just because we wanted to see them. My delusion receded with the nothing of interest staring us in the face. We could've gone this way or that, but instead it was Mom who suggested a retreat to whence we came, concluding our entire three minute Nob Hill experience. Back down the mountain we went to find electric restored and the museum re-open for business. Even with the momentary hiccup in our plan we managed to pick up right where we left off.

Roaming through the museum, I got my hands on cables, a car itself, and a variety of thing-ama-jigs to get a good feel for how it all worked. I was intrigued as I listened to descriptions of old time photos and informational boards read to me. Then I found my favorite spot of all, which happened to be the noisiest, at least when I was there. A genuine cable car bell was set up and ready for ringing. Impossible to resist, like I even tried, I grabbed hold of the chain and gave the sucker a tug. The clanging ding was loud, exceedingly so. My enthusiasm and its easy action collided, resulting in an ear piercing body jumping bell tone. My approach was far more gentle the second time round, and for each that followed. Giddy with the ringing delight, I came this close to buying the whole contraption in the gift shop. My thought, it could be our doorbell. Fortunately though for Kim and our neighbors, the cable bell was rather on the costly side and prevented such a purchase.

Kim too was having the time of her life in the cable car museum. Taking everything in, she reads signs, studies pictures and display items, and revels in all that is offered. As a result of her thoroughness and zeal, it never fails, Kim is always somewhere well behind. I may refer to it as dawdling, but in actuality, her curiosity and ability to appreciate are some of her wonderful attributes. With all this said, Kim dawdled about the museum while we waited and wondered what on earth could she possibly be doing. We three less pokey people realized it was the end of the line for our visit among the cable cars. Kim finally collected, we continued on with the rest of our day's plans.

THE ORIENT EXPRESSION

Who needs to go all the way to China to experience this wonderful Asian culture? I would like to suggest a jaunt to San Francisco's Chinatown for a far more convenient immersion. Its beginnings in the mid 1800's were anything but easy with all the anti-Chinese laws

Laura E. Walker

limiting and prohibiting their immigration. However, when China became allies to the US efforts during World War II, the "keep out" legislation was finally lifted and led to a booming surge. Today, San Francisco's Chinatown is the oldest Chinese community in America, and the largest in the world outside of China.

Even though we had intentionally planned to check out Chinatown, all that ensued was almost accidental in our touring. We tripped into this Asian environment in search of a bite to eat. I'm telling you, if the fates don't guide us, our bellies surely will. Trying to pick out a Chinese restaurant in Chinatown is like trying to pick out the best piece of hay in a stack of them. Our narrowing method became, we'll go into the one right in front of us. Not necessarily the best approach, but with the Great Oriental Restaurant now serving, it worked for us.

The compact restaurant was filled with circular tables crowded together with many small loud speaking indigenous people around each. I couldn't help but feel conspicuous as I navigated into the tight space, and not for the usual reasons either. Typically it's my cane which draws attention, but for a change the stick out was related to me and my family's stature. Blessed with a gene pool of tall chromosomes, our towering white selves stood easily head and shoulders above our dining companions. Not only did I collapse my cane at the table, but I had to fold my own frame just to fit in my seat.

Before the tiny hostess lady departed, she uttered a couple of words to our cozy gathered selves, "dim sum." As is so often the case in communicating, if meaning is not understood, the message won't get delivered. A point that is well exampled by our situation. I thought it was our hostess wishing us some kind of friendly Chinese bon appetite-like expression. Kim thought with the earlier power outages in this neighborhood that they were trying to clean out the kitchen by moving some food before it went bad sort of thing. Sarah never heard dim sum at all; instead she only could hear chicken fried rice from the voices inside her own head. Meanwhile, Mom, ever dutiful to our well-being, asked for a round of waters, speaking both distinctly and loudly in the doing so.

You may already be aware how communication manifests itself by many means. The most common being the verbal language and sound. What may be lesser known is that body language is more telling. Observation, awareness, or simply having a clue all are a part of effective communication as well. I say this to fill you in on something. We sucked at this communication thing.

Besides language being a true barrier with English not even a second one for the folks in this crowd, we also failed to observe the going-ons of our surroundings. We continued to stupidly cling to what we knew, English and menu food. Had we stopped for even a moment we might've noted the small servers who repeatedly approached our table and stated something quite incomprehensible as they presented a platter of food. But no, we were too focused on them understanding us, rather than trying to comprehend what was happening around us. We continued our not so subtle attempts to remind them we wanted to order off the menu by flapping and pointing at the plastic cover. Eventually the blank faced girls gave up on us and walked away, while we were left to wonder if we got across our meaning.

I can't exactly say when realization hit about this Chinese food delivery system. Maybe it was after the eighth approach of offered foods. Or, maybe it was the some thirty minutes we waited to actually give our order. Possibly it was my mother's glancing about and noticing the servers going table to table, and patrons sometimes taking what were before them. Whatever it was, we finally understood this was a walking Chinese buffet!

We finally got it and started saying yes to everything they brought before us. Especially since we weren't sure if the off the menu ordering took. Accepting this noodley thing and that fried yummy, we hungrily agreed this was the best whatever we ever ate. And then, oh my God, it came too, our ordered food. Huge mounds of Chinese deliciosities were brought on serving platter sized plates. Sarah was barely visible behind her pile of fried rice. My shrimp and Chinese vegetables was a bountiful harvest of amazingly fresh flavors. Kim and Mom lo meined and fu younged through whatever they ordered, only to have tons of it remain sitting on their plates. Each of us knew we certainly weren't gonna haul around Chinese doggie boxes the rest of the day, so we earnestly attacked the food equivalent of Mount Fuji. Wait, that's Japanese. I'll just say, our left overs could've stretched out the Great Wall of China a bit further.

Sitting back and hoping we might be able to still breathe, or for that matter, move, our little party had a few moments to take in the sights and sounds before the check arrived. I've gotta say, the Chinese language appears to my western ears to be an exaggerated, sing song way of speaking. Apparently we all thought this way, because none of us could stifle a giggle when we heard those little servers taking the food around and announcing what they had. Kim, having the uncanny ability to parrot, nailed it when she mimicked and translated it perfectly into English. Without a doubt, the stretched sung sounds were, "You fall down, and it's okay." Slam that phrase together, add a Chinese lilt, drag out the last bit, and it'll be spot on Chinese-ish. "Ufaldown,eets sokay. We were unable to hold onto decorum or anything resembling political correctness. Totally cracking up, our new found phrase became our slogan for the rest of the trip.

Our stuffed and bloated beyond comfort selves, were uncaring that a fortune cookie didn't come with the meal. What did arrive though was the check. Ignorance can be quite costly, as was our meal, yet a valuable lesson was learned. Pay attention for Pete's sake, or you'll be paying big time instead at the cash register.

Now with a taste of Chinatown bulging our belts, it was time to walk it off with a wander. I could hear one of the most common sounds associated with Asian music playing down the block, and interest had me heading for it. It was some sort of stringed instrument, sounding very similar to a violin—in pain. Following my ears, we located the source, and I made inquiry. This Chinese stringed instrument played with bow is called an Erhu. Spelled phonetically, that would be Ee Woo. Curiosity getting the best of me, as it normally does, I asked if I could "see" it for myself. The little old musician obliged my indulgence, by thrusting bow into my hand, and jerking both back and forth between the strings. I have to say, considering I had less than a nanosecond to figure this thing out, I sounded awfully good. It seems it's not at all difficult to replicate the noise of a screeching cat.

I quickly learned I can appreciate the music of an Erhu, mostly from a distance. I also learned, as with any instrument, the ability of its musician can enhance or diminish the level of enjoyment. For a bit down the street was another Erhu player, and he, even when close up, sounded much more accomplished and easier on the ear. Fascination not yet finished, I inquired where an Erhu could be purchased. Mom feared I really wanted one, but my thought was of furthering my tactile need. I hadn't the chance to touch the instrument enough to paint an accurate mental picture.

Around the corner lay another world music store, and in it, Erhus. Locating one, I sat with it on my lap and realized its simple design. The can shaped chamber at the base amplified the sound created by the bow drawn between the strings on the neck. Variation in tone was accomplished by finger placement and angling the bow. I admit to knowing basically nothing about playing an instrument requiring a bow, or any instrument for that matter, but I associated the Erhu with a cello. Maybe it's a distant cousin of sorts.

My caterwauling was interrupted by the far more melodious and pleasing tones of a Tongue Drum. Sarah discovered the hollow wooden box-like beauty and thumped on it, despite the sign advising against this action. Gorgeous in its resonance and kindred to drums, yet similar to the tonal range of bells, it caught both our fancy with the chiming wooden quality. I was enchanted and might've been persuaded in its purchase, had I a few hundred dollars extra in my pocket. Needless to say, I don't, and I didn't.

LOMBARD STREET

In proclaiming its very unstraight status, the Lombard Sayers do not quibble with clarification. Previous to our San Franciscan visit, I had erroneously believed the entire length of Lombard was all wavy and such, but I quickly learned it was not. Our hotel occupied a spot on the same street, miles away from the famous section, and was as direct as they come. Inquiring, I learned the famous crooked portion of this street is confined to a single block. However, this brevity should not detract from the need to experience this short stretch of bent pavement.

Our intrepid troop had trudged for miles to connect with Lombard Street. Since its stretch ran from the Presidio to the Embarcadero, we believed it best to reference the map again to determine the correct direction. I remain perplexed to this day on the matter of our constant upward mobility. In that, we were always heading up something while in San Francisco. How this is possible is beyond me, for the laws of physics and geography had to have us at the top of a hill, street, or stairs, yet we never seemed to be. And so we went with our approach to Lombard's twisted way.

Nobody talks about it. It doesn't have tourist T-shirts and postcards immortalizing its unique attributes. It is the red headed step child of roads. Let me do my best to change all that by introducing Lombard Street's Block Before. Unraveled and unaided in any way, I swear the Block Before's relentless incline had to be at least ninety degrees. The unforgiving ascent was truly the greatest challenge of our entire trip. It may stand in the shadow of its upper section and not have the lavish frills and doting followers, but if it weren't for the Block Before's being, there wouldn't be no fancy-pants Lombard Street to visit. Just you remember that.

Standing at the base of the famous Lombard section, the need to weave the street quickly became obvious. The twenty-seven degree slope was made clear to me when Sarah took my finger and pointed it up to the hill's crest. Unnatural for neighborhoods to be settled on such a tilt, the Russian Hill money makers found the solution when one of its residents suggested a switchback approach to the road. Gradual angles of decline were humanly installed by switching the street back and forth in direction. This has permitted a do-able and safe descent for those wishing to traverse the hill ever since the 1920's.

Sidewalks and stairs line either side of the street and is the recommended means for tourists on foot to experience the hill. To be honest, I think it might be a law or something. I understand pedestrians are not needed as an additional obstacle on this course, while vehicles negotiate the 5mph descent. However Sarah interpreted the sidewalk law as optional, and guided me right up the curvy street. The rationale, how else was I going to get a feel for it.

Boldly going where we shouldn't have been, Sarah led me up. Each elevated step and the frequent change of direction provided a mobile mapping of the road beneath my feet. I'm grateful Sarah dared to non-conform for our path less taken did allow a better understanding. The impression of beautiful flowers lining walls and homes amidst Rock and greenery was not lost on me, and combined to make a most scenic scape on my mind's eye. The ascent on Lombard was a chore, but honestly, it wasn't as horrible as I thought it could be. This was probably due to my frequent use of the incline on my treadmill, or more likely, all the stops for photo ops that we took.

It's amazing to think people actually live on this section of street, having to wrangle through the throngs of site seers and the hill itself, just to get into their driveway. Aesthetically pleasing, naturally challenging, Lombard Street's famed side winding section of road was worth the effort both in finding it, as well as climbing it. And after our naps, we finally believed it.

ALCATRAZ PRISON

The name alone conjures up thoughts of murderous criminals, bleak isolation, and inescapable confinement. What better place for a family vacation visit I say. The idea of taking a night time tour of the infamous Rock was enthusiastically pitched to Mom, and underwhelmingly received. Never a fan of prison stories, the poor woman has been subjected to mob and incarceration movies over the years due to her marriage to my father. His affinity for such things and control of the remote has left her haplessly watching. Coercion never applied, yet some amounts of coaxing were, Mom reluctantly agreed to go to the island. She'd see about the prison once there.

The infamous Alcatraz prison has been immortalized and celebrated in the annals of history as the most heinous incarceration facility in the

United States. Its brief twenty-nine years of operation, from 1934 to 1963, saw the likes of Al Capone, Machine Gun Kelly, and countless other nefarious bad boys of the day hold up within its walls. Considered the prison system's prison, Alcatraz was a maximum security minimum privilege institution, providing only the most basic of rights to the inmates. Food, clothing, shelter, and medical treatment were given; anything else had to be earned.

The mystique and hardened lore of the Rock make for an irresistible draw when it comes to the movies. Hollywood has captivated audiences with stories loosely based on truths. Accuracy not necessarily the point as much as good story telling, a murderous felon becomes the gentled Bird Man, and championed are the escapes. Not to be outdone, the National Park Service has profited greatly from the Alcatraz allure as well. Open since 1973 to tourists, the former prison facility has become one of the most visited in the country. Site restoration continues, and will provide even greater access to those seeking a piece of history from the Rock.

Night tour booked and one short ferry ride later, we landed on the normally blustering cold island of Alcatraz. Fortunate for the freeze babies in our midst, the tepid climate wasn't present. However, the squawking bay gulls were. Hatchling season apparently turns these normally foraging creatures into loud protective nesters. Duly warned about the chilly island climate and the steep ascent to the prison, we were now informed by our park ranger tour guide these ferocious fowls were federally protected. I think they knew it too.

The walk past the gull guards and up to the prison entrance was made interesting by the park ranger's educating talk. The path we took was partially built by inmates who had earned the privilege of working. Monotonous restrictions within the prison walls and the opportunity to be outside even made back breaking labor preferred. We entered Alcatraz prison through the same entrance new convicts were brought in, and all similarities between tourist and prisoner ended there.

Stepping into the confined darkened room we tourists were greeted warmly by another park ranger. The prisoner's welcome was a little less cordial as the guards ordered them to strip and ready themselves for a rather thorough search, of which I am not compelled to detail in the least. We visitors were handed equipment for a self-guiding narration of the facility as we entered the shower room. Dignity removed for the inmates, as well as any ill placed contraband, they were given a bar of soap. Tourists fanned out and meandered through the cell block, casually stopping to take in a particular point of interest. The new inmates carried issued uniforms as they marched buck naked straight down Broadway to a rousing chorus of cat-calls and jeers.

I was blown away by the incredible audio narration of the Alcatraz tour. Former guards and inmates shared their stories while convincing sound effects were added to enhance the telling. I actually felt as though I was there when it was a working prison and even removed my headphones to figure out if someone was blowing a whistle to get my attention. Hearing the voices of those who lived on Alcatraz, whether as a result of punishment or eking out a living brought an incredible authenticity and realism to touring the facility. The conveniences of stopping the audio when a certain something required an extra look-see, or just being able to rewind a portion made the experience extremely user friendly.

I entered into the small cell of solitary and felt its confinement bear down on me. Captivated by his story, I listened to an inmate speak of his time served, and literally I could hear and feel the cold bleakness. I had the privilege of an open cell door, but those sent to solitary were entombed in darkness. One prisoner spoke of his attempts to occupy his mind by tearing off a button from his uniform. Tossing it, he played an endless game of hide and seek. Keeping hold of sanity was achieved by individual effort, but for some, it was not enough.

Alcatraz's facility was fascinating, but to be truthful, I had anticipated a far more dismal, dungeonesque quality in its appearance. Admittedly I was taking it in as a tourist, a blind one to boot, so it's likely it was considerably drearier when in use. I realize the cells were small and the inmates practically slept with heads in the toilet, but at least daylight was visible from large windows along the top. Emptied now, the library was huge, and once held shelves of approved reading materials. The year round damp weather and the menacing inmate population surely made for awful living conditions, but I was expecting crude devices of torture, dank, dripping hallways, and a rat or two still running around.

Trying to gather people together to leave is difficult enough when they want to go, but when departure is less preferred to the staying, the process is much like herding cats. Tourists all over the Rock and the last ferry of the night readying to ship out, our park ranger hosts resorted to enticement to get us all gone. Stragglers shooed and rear hemmed in, a loud speaking ranger gave a lesson on the famous escape attempts of Alcatraz.

Touted for its inescapability, Alcatraz inmates gave it the old prison break try time and time again. Some attempts were well planned, but the telling of my personal favorite emphasized different qualities. A couple of guys named Doc Barker and Rufus managed to get out of the cellblock, get past the guards, and down to the water's edge all without detection. Not bad for amateur escapers really, however here is where the debacle begins. For whatever reason, Rufus had failed to disclose a somewhat relevant fact, he couldn't swim; a point which is rather significant considering they were imprisoned on an island.

I could only garner a guess as to their state of emotion as the sun was about to rise, the inmate headcount beginning, and that their jig would soon be up unless they made way into the water. One thing I'd put money on though, loving platitudes probably weren't exchanged. Adhering to some unwritten prison code of ethics, or possibly the no break buddy left behind rule, Doc remained loyal and took pity on Rufus' swimming impairment. Grabbing what was available, they set about to build a raft from shoreline debris. As imagined, this sort of thing may require some time and know-how, of which they had neither.

Needless to say, the morning wake up ritual at Alcatraz alerted the guards of the missing felons. The sun soon burned off the remaining darkness of night along with the fog blanketing the island, and revealed our boys going nowhere fast. A good effort made, but with nothing to show for it, maybe it's we who can benefit from a take away lesson here. The first of which comes to mind, don't break the law and end up in jail. If you do, consider the location of said prison and adjust all break-out plans accordingly. Don't ever partner up with a guy named Rufus. And by all means, communicate. Spend a little quality time getting to know the felon you're seeking your freedom with. Go ahead, make that list of their strengths, weaknesses, and what they have to offer the whole escape experience. I'm sure Doc would suggest the same, now.

Our time on Alcatraz was all to brief. Something I'm sure the former residents never thought. I don't often speak of regrets, primarily because I don't usually have any, but with this visit I do. I would have liked to explore more, take a walk around and get my hands on things to see the prison better. I would have enjoyed taking the beneath Alcatraz tour and roaming the island to appreciate the terrain. I would have picked the brains of the wonderful park rangers to learn more of the daily life upon the Rock. These kinds of regrets are easily remedied with a return visit to Alcatraz Island, something I hope to do in the nearer future. In the meantime, I will apprehend my regret and sentence myself to a promise of much more time on the Rock.

MYTH-CONCEPTION MENDING

Tucked into my brain's recesses were a few bits and pieces of information about Alcatraz's notorious prison history. Most of which had been put there by movies I had watched. Between the audio presentation and the well versed, knowledgeable park rangers willing to chat, my mind reeled. I heard tell slightly altered tales and realized myth-conceptions needed mending.

The Bird Man Of Alcatraz:

Robert Stroud was never once the man of birds while serving his time on the Rock. The pet name was bestowed when incarcerated at Leavenworth. Believing his canary hobby to be constructive, the prison officials permitted Stroud his studies, until contraband and a homemade distillery were discovered. Transferred to Alcatraz in 1942 after killing a couple of fellow cell buddies, Stroud never had his feathered roommates again. A cantankerous killer and uncooperative in real life, Stroud's rehabilitation never came close to the mild mannered Burt Lancaster persona in the movie.

Laura E. Walker

At Home On The Rock:

Be it ever so humble, Alcatraz Island was home to more than the inmates of its prison. The guards and their families also lived on the island in a small residential community. Wives and children went about their daily business in the shadow of gun towers and the great stone wall. Taking the ferry daily to attend school in San Francisco, the children often would make the return trip home with incoming prisoners. With Alcatraz literally being a rock island, groceries, supplies, and fresh water all had to be ferried across the bay.

Shark Waters:

Alcatraz's inescapable reputation was built upon a few natural factors. This island made of rock, surrounded by frigid rapid flowing waters, filled with man-eating sharks a mile or so from land was perfect for keeping those nasty felons in their places. As is so often the case with reputations, it can become quite askew depending on the information getting out. Take for instance the shark infested waters of San Francisco. The only thing swimming out there that enjoys meat is the wind surfing swimming athlete types, and most are probably vegetarians. The species of sharks inhabiting the bay are anything but people eating, for they feed off the bottom. Talk of sharks probably kept the prisoners put, but more likely it was the difficult swim they couldn't handle. Unlike inmates today who have many luxuries by comparison, Alcatraz's occupants lacked nutritious meals, regular exercise, and simply weren't aware of what lay beyond the walls holding them.

Escape Escapades:

Escapes are probably what dreams are made of, at least for most any prison population, but especially so for the Alcatraz fellows. Fourteen times it was attempted, and legend has it all have failed. Any number of methods were used to get-away, from the traditional filing through the bars to acquiring piece by piece a military uniform and leaving with the troops. Probably the best known and most ingenious was the smuggling of rubber raincoats to make a raft. Of the 36 men who attempted escape, five are listed as missing and presumed dead, their bodies never found.

It's possible one of those guys did make it to freedom, nobody will ever really know, but until proven otherwise, Alcatraz's inescapable record remains intact.

THE GREAT REDWOOD FOREST

Nearly in unison with the decision to visit San Francisco was my declaration, "I want to see the Redwoods!" Mind you, I hadn't a clue where to find these giant trees, only knowing California had some somewhere. My geographic ignorance notwithstanding, I soon learned a surviving grove resided just north of the bay, and Muir Woods became our destination.

Before we step into the woods, I thought setting the historical scene might be interesting. America was changing with the industrial revolution in full swing. People were more spread out than ever, and making a mess everywhere. President Teddy Roosevelt was the guy in charge and a real man's man. His rough and tumble outdoorsy ways demonstrated his love for the land as much as the opportunity to go hunt and kill something on it. Congressman William Kent was also a land loving, tree hugging sort, so much so that he purchased a huge portion of it in California to preserve its being. Then along came a group of money makers wanting to dam up a nearby river, which would've caused mass flooding and the destruction of a particular area of Redwoods on the Kent land. Knowing it would be years of legal battles, Congressman Kent usurped the process and slipped neatly through a loophole. His donation of the land in order to save this pristine place was complete when given to the government. President Roosevelt thusly declared it a national monument, preserving it as is, and the dam boys probably uttered a few same sounding expletives with their loss. Monuments of course need naming, and the obvious choice was to entitle it after its benefactor, however Mr. Kent suggested otherwise. Putting forth the notion of the woods honoring the naturalist John Muir, who had been instrumental in the development of the national park system, the beautiful forest land is now known as Muir Woods.

Securing a private tour for our visit to the Redwoods had us up very early in the morning—the reason being, an unofficial visit to the park.

Certain hours are kept at national monuments, and it was our plan to not observe them. Usually my inner voice will divert any devious ideas into rightness. If that's not working, there's always Sarah and Kim who assert reason and sometimes fear to do what is correct. But on this morning, nobody was speaking up. We all wanted in before the crowds of bus tourists came flocking in to trample the peace.

Excited anticipation had my adrenalin coursing through my body. I think I leaped from my seat upon arrival, but most likely not. Standing there, waiting to enter, I knew I had to slow myself down, and my mind, or I would race through and not truly experience the ancient evergreens waiting before me. In the few steps taken to the entrance, I silently made my requests known.

The cool crisp air settled over me, clinging to my body. I could feel myself being drawn and absorbed into the stillness of the great woods. I felt present in the presence of the life around me. The soft quiet barely moving on the chilled air. The giants themselves give comfort from their strength and longevity. The canopy towered into the heavens as bright sunlight filtered through, glorious and warm, streaming down onto that which lay below. The new, small beginnings. The gentle stirring of water flowing, seeking, waiting. I felt securely surrounded and in a place of greatness. This was truly a wondrous sanctuary created by life and time.

The great Redwoods have spanned the centuries, ever growing, ever being. Roots networked among its family, a tree will bear acorns and the generations to follow begin their process by surrounding its elder. This family, known as a fairy circle, will grow and enmesh with the rooted support system established. Thriving and sustained, it is a family whose inheritance is a gift to us. Our human span on this earth is brief, yet it is we who threaten the existence of these long living entities. My thoughts of well-being and hope mingled with the essence and life forces surrounding me, and I was, and am, deeply grateful to have met that which is far greater than I.

The moments spent in Muir Woods were wonderful. I had time to appreciate the beauty around me and could feel a synergy exist. I stopped often to touch the immensity of the Redwoods. Wrapping my arms as best I could; I tree hugged. My arm span was not even close to being enough to embrace the trunk. I rapped on the bark surface fascinated by the hollow sound answering my knuckles. Bark protecting the core within, encasing gently, the wooden skin blanketed itself.

We joined a chorus of inhabitants, a guest in their home. A silent yet present small resident was the Banana Slug. The slimy, cold insect was disgustingly fascinating as I dared to hold one. A narrow brook contributed its gentle melody to the sound of the wood, and home to the salmon swimming upstream to spawn. Birds added their improvised harmonies as the great trees whispered with soft sounds of life. Quietly deer foraged through the undergrowth, adding percussion from footfall upon pieces of wood unable to remain whole. Infinite was this Music, and at its most natural.

I am a person greatly taken with history, its lessons, people, and stories. I am also confounded by the concept of time, whether by length or the possibility of traveling in and through it. This place, among the Redwoods, became the culmination of both curiosities. Being in this forest was a walk back into the ages. Trees withstanding the test of time have been the living witnesses to what has preceded us. These testaments began their life journey in mankind's designated first century, some even further beyond. They are living trees spanning the changes of the world and the results of humanity. I try to grasp this notion with my limited viewpoint, but it is too grand a concept to completely hold onto.

I was amazed by the simple display of a section of Redwood from a fallen tree some seventy years prior. Representing the passage of its life time, the ring lines are marked with mankind's history simultaneous to a year in the life of this tree. Such occurrences as Columbus sailing the Atlantic and America's declaration of independence were given examples. Events monumentally significant in the formation of human civilization were but merely a passing moment for this ever green being.

My complete self, mind, body, and spirit were enriched by our visit to the Redwoods. With gratitude and hope I say, longer may they live.

THE CASTRO

The very essence of San Francisco lies in its many varied neighborhoods and can be defined by the ethnicity, culture, and beliefs of the people living within. As people come and go, so to do the influences and characteristics of these areas, inevitably changing the face of the community. No better example is there than the Castro district.

Once known as Eureka Valley, its renaming is attributed to the popular theater in its midst. The Castro saw many changes in its people during the twentieth century. Formerly a Scandinavian community, then an Irish working class neighborhood, the Castro's gay influx began during World War II. The U.S. military discharging of "homosexuals" landed these servicemen in San Francisco. Unable to return home, they found each other and community in the Castro. This famed gayborhood is known today for the turbulent political revolution of the 70's, the openly gay activist and politician Harvey Milk, and the beginning of civil rights for all peoples.

Kim and I were inspired to visit this rainbow clad spot after watching the documentary, "The Life and Times of Harvey Milk." Leaving Mom and Sarah behind to attend to girly things like mani-petis, we lit out in search of the big gay-dom.

Our first site to be seen was the home and work place of Mr. Milk, the Castro Camera Shop. Thing is, we hadn't taken the time to figure out the address beforehand and had to rely on the kindness of strangers to point us in the correct direction. Locating it on the main drag, so to speak, Kim and I took a moment to read the inscribed plaque in the sidewalk out front. Had we been standing there some thirty years prior, Harvey most likely would've recruited us to work on one of his campaigns, and get out the word on the need for equality. Instead, we silently lifted our thanks to the loud mouthed charismatic hippy living manic visionary for all he did during his brief life upon this earth.

Altogether different than its 70's appearance, the new century occupants were of a slightly higher caliber. Or so they thought. Kim and I dared to wander around the shop hoping to feel the former vibe. Items crafted by artists and a vase out of my financial bracket, I kept my hands and stick to myself as I held my breath. Incapable of absorbing the milieu of history due to sticker shock and oxygen deprivation, I gratefully exited the building. Relief was my only emotion, not even a lick of appreciative nostalgia in me.

Meandering about the streets, it had to be obvious even to those gaydarless that this was a G-spot. G of course meaning gay. Rainbow this and that's, assorted reading materials including three newspapers dedicated to the gay agenda and lifestyle, and gay men everywhere, provided just some of the clues. Kim and I popped in and out of shops, working our way down to the train station and the hugest rainbow flag ever; may it wave. This colorful flag shone brightly against a backdrop of blue sky, as it blustered about on the winds. Not in the least bit subtle, it may only be outdone by the Castro home painted top to bottom in the colors of the rainbow.

Intentionally making the change from light hearted activities to a more solemn one is not necessarily ideal when on vacation, but sometimes it's simply the right thing to do. And so Kim and I set out to find a special memorial dedicated to gay individuals whose lives were prematurely ended. The pink inverted triangle is embraced today by the gay community at large as a symbol of solidified identity. However its initial intent was sinister, and represented loathing and bigotry at its worst in history. The Nazi concentration camps were not exclusive ones, for they held captive and exterminated more than the Jewish people. Anyone who was deemed different in the eyes of the Arian master race was rounded up as well, and gay men were quickly and quietly targeted. They too were branded with identifying marks, the pink inverted triangle, to represent their perceived crime. In memory of those gay individuals put to death during that horrifying time, a monument was established in the Castro, and Kim and I both felt the need to pay our respects.

The park garden was not a quiet, peaceful place as I had anticipated, since surrounded by roads and traffic, but somehow this seemed appropriate. For the time it represented, and the inhumanities committed, were neither quiet nor peaceful. Respecting the past and reflecting the present, individual monoliths were sculpted into inverted triangles and shaded softly with pink at the pinnacle. Each smooth pillar of granite designated some 1,000 persons extinguished in the camps. I remember asking Kim to tell me how many of them were there, and I waited, listening.

I could hear her whispers as she softly counted, turning to face each column. My thoughts unwitting to believe as I listened to the number grow. One, two, three . . . the whispers of thousands. Eight, nine . . . this many, how can this be? Eleven . . . pain and disgust for the unknown and forgotten. Fourteen, fifteen . . . enough . . . too many.

Fifteen-thousand recorded individuals, spirits of life were obliterated because of prejudice and hate. Even still, so many more since, and I felt cold inside. I turned my thoughts outward, asking, pleading, such ignorance and intolerable hatred would not again be allowed—to anyone.

I collected a few pink hued stones from the garden path, wanting to take a piece of this place with me. Even more, I want to remember what has happened before me, and a reminder of what I personally must do. Being true to one's self may not always be easy, yet the time I now live in cannot be compared to what others have experienced before me. My personal struggles do not involve the threat of my life being taken. I will not fully comprehend this kind of fear, yet I at times live with my own worries of rejection. Comparisons nowhere near equal, but real nonetheless. I have promised myself I will strive to remain true, wanting to honor both my being and those who have given so greatly before me.

The solemn feeling we had experienced in this little garden place slowly dissipated as we departed. Winding up in front of the historic Castro Theater, Kim excitedly suggested we go have a peek. The purchase of two tickets for the double feature B movies of the 80s, Little Darlings and Meatballs, got us into a sure pick me up. Not exactly Academy material back then, they certainly hadn't gained any strength over the decades. Somehow though, seeing these incredibly dated flicks, or at least parts of them, became a delightful stroll down nostalgia lane. What I couldn't believe is how much the crackling hiss and pops of the old films made me happy. Oh sure, quality surround digitized mega sound could be had with any new movie these days, but the classic hum of celluloid working its way through a projector was wonderful, and something I didn't even realize I missed.

Despite the warm happy feelings elicited from watching the movies, we weren't really there for that. The Castro Theater was constructed and opened in 1922 at a cost of $300 thousand, a big chunk of change for the times. Lavishly decorated in blah blah blah, how the hell do I know, the thing was old, a titch gaudy, but grand nonetheless. Seating capacity once near 1400, the cavernous room held far less on this night. Yet each person there was enthusiastic with opportunity and anticipation.

Kim and I wandered around the lobby, taking in old photos, feeling antiquated projectors of film, and generally soaking up the atmosphere. Stopping to read articles written about the theater's opening was a hoot, so much so that this particular line deserves notation:

"Usherettes, schooled in the art of feminine tact, will greet the patrons at the opening." (*Eureka Valley Herald*, June 22, 1922.)

I too was similarly schooled, learning not to scratch myself in public. Always remembering to sit like a lady even if my sweaty thighs keep slipping apart. Don't dig out my bra from under my boobs no matter how hot it is unless I'm sure I won't be caught. Other such tidbits remain, however due to the personal nature of them, I don't feel it appropriate to mention. I wouldn't want my faux pas to be social now. DISCLAIMER: Doris Walker, mother of this writer, did her best and is in no way responsible for Laura's views on femininity or the acts therein.

During the movie intermission, Kim and I moved about the inner sanctum of this grand theater. Reminiscent of a red carpeted debut

145

and a photo op royale, were the many flashes from Kim's snap happy ways all over the place. The movie screen was shrouded with large hanging curtains, drawn closed until start and were slowly cast open when ready. As in the by-gone days of cinema, a gentleman entertained us with standards played upon a Wurlitzer pipe organ. I couldn't have kept from smiling if I wanted to, for fascination and thrill collided as I sat there taking in the wonderful sounds of this magnificent instrument. Chimes, trumpets, and many luscious notes were skillfully played until musician and instrument gently descended below the flooring. It was awesome and made me realize why folks from the day use to get all dressed up when going out to catch a flick. It was quite the event. Yet being a 21st century gal, I will never give up my casual clothed comforts.

I really wasn't sure what to expect when Kim and I decided to go to the Castro. To be honest, it's probably best. Pre-conceived notions often get in the way, and may spoil the real experience. From the emotion felt in a tiny garden, to the delight of early days revisited, each filled me well. Homage now paid to the Castro, Kim and I will not soon forget this wonderful little neighborhood at the end of the rainbow.

GOLDEN GATE PARK

Literally wanting to spend some of our last hours on the tippy edge of the west coast, we headed straight for the beach. Golden Gate Park was our destination, the Pacific Ocean our goal, and a public bus the means to accomplish both. But first, how.

Mom once again took out her handy dandy map picked up on the first day and now well-worn from excessive use. She studied the streets and bus lines and concluded the best approach. Reciting confidently, she mentioned this route and that, and we were ready for it, proud of her navigational skills even. Until the desk clerk said, "No, just go out front and catch the bus, it'll take you right there." Oh sure knowledgeable show off, why be easy if you can be difficult? Yet we heeded his recommendation merely because of time constraints.

Golden Gate Park holds miles of acres, and fortunately for us, our plans included a minutia of them. Instead we shuttled on down to the shoreline, heading for the sea like baby turtles migrating across sand. It may not have been the most graceful water approach, but we got there unscathed and ready to dip toes into the Pacific blue.

I was excited about this encounter with a new body of water and entered with all due enthusiasm. For a nanno-second that is. Holy crap, it was unbelievably cold! I mean, I knew it was going to be chilly, but wasn't really ready for this much frigidness. The icy salt water stung my tender toes, forcing me to yelp from shock. Less eager upon second approach, I was more steadfast in my resolve to conquer the cold, and did so, at least by the sixth attempt. Whether it was grim determination, or simply my extremities had gone numb, it ultimately didn't matter. I was in the Pacific Ocean.

Far less gleeful about these deep waters is our land loving Sarah. Not yet quite recovered from her off Mexico snorkeling expedition of 2004, she continues to have less than fond feelings towards the ocean, and prefers to admire it from afar—like Kansas. Ever the trooper, and not really having a choice in the matter, she summed up the courage to guide me across the beach. I thought at first Sarah was dallying as she scanned the sands for sea given trinkets. Turns out, I was right. However the good from that became, Sarah's keen eyesight netted her wonderful treasures, from an intact sand dollar, to nifty rocks. Mind you, that dollar of sand was priceless, seeing how it is incredibly fragile and survived the pounding surf as well as crunching feet to land whole in Sarah's hand.

Developing a shoreline clench upon my arm, Sarah managed to set reluctant foot into the water. She too did not initially last long, but with confidence growing, and the cold water soothing her hot feet, she realized it wasn't so bad. The water had barely reached beyond her ankles, but let's not diminish the achievement. I see no future in oceanography for Sarah, but reducing the primordial fear previously experienced is certainly a step in the right direction to tolerance at least.

The remaining two of our party were equally content to be visiting the Pacific. Neither of them were fearful, rather they delighted and soaked up the beauty before them, each in their own way. Mom cast her gaze over the waters, drawing in the scenic colors and the illusion of distant mountains upon the horizon. Billowy fog on the ocean surface was the reality, yet no less beautiful than what she had perceived. Kim's appreciation captured on film and memory, she basked in the joys shared with nature's gift, our thrill, and the amusement of nearby dogs freely playing.

As previously mentioned, Golden Gate Park is quite large. We had in hand a much-needed map which covered a thousand acres or so of its contents. Extraordinary, bordering on the bizarre, items were available for the viewing such as real live buffalo. Among the more customary findings were a variety of gardens, ponds to fish, music venues, and a place to observe the heavens. Somewhere in the in between, Mom came across the rose garden and stated her desire to have a gander at these beauties. You'd think this would be an innocent enough request.

Fragrant flowers in varying states of bloom, and even greater variety of colors, welcomed us into the garden. I sniffed my way through, while the rest visually appreciated the elegance before them. Finding favorites with names like Glowing Peace, Mom wandered happily along. What joyous contentment there was among the lovely roses.

Mom walked blissfully from rosebush to next, drawn by color and flowering fashion. Seeking the next bit of beauty, she looked ahead and caught a glimpse of something, something unfamiliar. Curiosity piqued, glance became intentional stare. "What is that?" I heard the words, but was too far behind to offer opinion, even if I could've seen it. As a hummingbird is drawn to sweet nectar, so to was Mom to that which captured her attention. Sidling up alongside, she discovered it was a surrey of sorts. A bicycle built for four.

Fascination and fun, Mom wanted to take a test drive. That's all I needed by way of encouragement, and was in the seat before anyone. Honestly, we knew this must've belonged to someone, and had no plans of stealing it, but the renter approached us to make sure on both counts.

Permission granted, we all piled in and giddily glided some 20 yards. That was it, we had to rent our own and set off to do so. Oh sure, we went the wrong direction, what's new with that? Premonition was once again ignored with familiarity and blind enthusiasm. Mission firmly planted in mind and fun in store, we wanted to ride.

It took great effort to find and rent a surrey, but we all were confident in its worth-whiledness and of the wonderful outing about to ensue. Saddled up and the thing ours for one hour, we set off with Kim as driver, I had shotgun, and the grand mother/daughter combo filled the rear. Oh the joy, rapture even as we flew as upon the wind, coasting effortlessly downhill. Oh the fear, terror even, as we sped quickly and ever nearer to the gated exit before us. Brakes not yet figured out, Kim pulled a Flintstone's stop and dragged rubbered soles across the ground to save us.

Now you'd think nearly colliding headlong into peril within the first minute of riding might've been a deterrent, but it was not. Sarah hopped out, removed said barrier, and onward we rode. Peddling became quite an interesting phenomenon in that at times legs and feet would be whirling around akin to a hamster on its wheel, while at other moments, we could hardly breathe from the exertion. Our moods were equally reflected with highs and lows, sheer joy giving in to disdain. And it was soon thereafter we put it all together and realized for each easy down, there was the anti; the butt-busting up. Our notions of a leisurely ride were replaced with the grueling and most sweaty reality of work. We were on the sorry surrey ride from hell.

Somehow the quiet paths once traveled became roads filled with motorized vehicles. There we were, four peddling fools, sweating, breathing heavily, and now, thoroughly lost. Despite the park map affixed to our surrey, we couldn't buy a clue as to where we were or how to be elsewhere. We peddled till hearts pounded and pulses raced. And we had only been on the darn thing 20 minutes! Lost, tired, a short respite was called for and granted. While the two map lovers, Mom and Kim, poured over directions and pointed here and there, I just went and lay on a park bench. Consensus reached and affirmed by unknown passer-byers, we headed in what was believed to be the right direction to return this doom cycle.

Down the road a bit, past the playground, we had to be getting close. Hope gleamed brightly on the horizon and each peddle thrust forward seemed to be easier than the last. An open downhill run lay before us and I spoke for the crew when saying, "This is the best part of the whole ride!" Swoosh! We soared upon surrey, and, right out of the park?

Adept directional sense had led us out the exit, through a busy intersection, and across four, count'em, four lanes of traffic. We were out on the open road now and quite unsure whether to laugh hysterically or be afraid. Fortunately some of us covered one emotion, while the rest picked up the other. I'll let you discern which got what. Immediately we pulled over realizing we were off the map and on uncharted surrey territory. That and, God help us, we were still heading down hill.

Turning around was no small feat, however it was managed despite continued giggles weakening half the group. As any good driver, we heeded the light at the intersection and managed to keep from rolling back down the hill. Tempers flared momentarily as seemingly unwarranted horn honking blasted our direction, but quickly we were alerted to Kim's wallet which had escaped and lay in the middle of the thoroughfare. Light changing to green, our senior member bounded from quad cycle, snatched up the precious possession, and hopped back in. What else, I ask you, what else could possibly go wrong on this alleged leisurely ride? Well momentum would be the short answer. By the time we picked ours up, we were barely half way over the four lanes, and the light glared down a menacing yellow at us.

Putting rubber to peddle, the four of us pumped our weary legs and generated enough speed to get us through, and back into the park we went. No less lost, we celebrated our return and life in general. Those few seconds of joy dissipated with the sudden awareness of the beast that lay before us. Remember that gleeful statement of the best part of the trip as we soared DOWN hill? Talk about your "coming back to bite us in the ass moment", sheesh. We attempted to peddle but got nowhere fast, expending all energy in just keeping ourselves from rolling backwards. Fed up and ready to abandon this evil vehicle by the side of the road, Mom commanded us "OUT!" We were pushing. Minus Kim, the most able bodied of us, who sat up front and steered while taking a phone call from her parents. Oh my God, the absurdity of it all!

Seemingly hours later, we finally crested the top and fell back into this vehicle, which appeared to be mocking us now. Course reset, I don't really recall the last minutes of our ride, or how we even got back to the rental booth, but we did. Ideas of fun replaced with the reality of fatigue, we dismounted and walked away not giving a damn we were some 20 minutes over the hour rental. Civil communication began shortly after the soothing ice cream sandwiches slid down our throats. Not until later, way later at the airport did we find the humor and began laughing raucously at our own idiocy. Determining a valuable lesson learned, we agreed next time, no roses for Mom.

THE GOLDEN GATE BRIDGE

We've seen it from a far, from below, and at 60 mph while crossing it, but it was now my turn to see the Golden Gate Bridge my way. The largest suspension bridge in the world glows brightly with the less than subtle International Orange it is painted. I wanted to experience it for myself, and the only way it was going to happen was by getting up close and personal.

The bus route we took to and from Golden Gate Park conveniently stopped at the bridge's base. We had no more than an hour to spare, so squeezing this last have-to from my list was definitely icing on the San Franciscan cake. Opened in 1937, the bridge was so named because it spanned the width of the bay, also known as the Golden Gate. I was excited to get my feet and hands on this iconic symbol of the city and hurried Sarah along. Sidewalk wide and filled to capacity with tourists, we managed to walk out on the bridge and over the water, not quite reaching halfway. Time being at a premium, I figured distance crossed was less important to me than getting a feel for the bridge's construction.

Laura E. Walker

A couple of things I immediately noticed while on the bridge were, first, the bright red 911 emergency phone. I have been a crisis hotline worker for years, and something like this quickly caught my attention. I began to wonder about those dire individuals thinking to use the bridge for another kind of crossing. I'm not about to begin citing statistics, instead I will only share the average of two people a month making the leap is a whole lot more than I ever had to contend with.

Standing on the bridge, I noted the surprising lack of movement. Suspension construction allowed for road shifting with the grouping of cables as it hung from a far larger cable above, which in turn was affixed to the towers. Obviously this is an over simplification of the technical aspects of the bridge, but it's the best I can figure out and store in my head. Basically, I conceptualize the bridge to be a massive swing-like contraption, allowing give and take of its driving surface. Since I had heard the bridge moves, I anticipated feeling it. I didn't, at least at first. Instead, I became aware of the vibrating hum of kinetic energy as I placed my hands on the cable support. I was intrigued and drawn to feeling many of the coiled strands hanging in groups of four.

I began to think of the vibration of the cable as the life force of the bridge. Like so many functions of a living body not observed, or simply taken for granted, I slowed myself to become aware of the bridge's energy. Grasping the woven metal with my hand, I moved fingers mindfully over each of the many smaller strands joined together to make the larger, and felt the tremulous motion all the while. Small made great, energies flowing and returning, unobserved unless aware, I spent an intentional moment with the awesome Golden Gate Bridge.

Not so much awed as she was AHHHed, Mom too had her moment with the bridge. The woman is quite unfond of high places and has occasional bouts of PTSD, stemming from high towers and little daughters peering over the edge, or something like that. Despite her phobic responses to elevation, Mom decidedly determined to conquer the bridge. Walking tall, and not near the rail, Doris Walker Superstar made her way. As I was mind melding with the bridge, Mom sucked it up and dared to peer over its side, and down. Down was a long way, yet Mom managed her high anxiety. I'm not saying she had fun doing all

152

this, but at least she can say she's walked the Golden Gate Bridge and lived to tell of her triumph.

Demonstrating the hugeness of the top cable from which all others suspend, a large piece of brightly painted coil was on display. Here is where I truly began to fathom the immensity of this entire structure and the intricacies of such a feat. The only word I had then to describe my thoughts were, "WOW!" Now I can slightly articulate myself better by saying, San Francisco has many wonderful iconic landmarks, but literally the Golden Gate Bridge stands above them all.

I LEFT MY HEART IN SAN FRANCISCO

High on a hill, it calls to me
To be where little cable cars
Climb halfway to the stars!
The morning fog may chill the air
I don't care!
My love waits there in San Francisco
Above the blue and windy sea
When I come home to you, San Francisco,
Your golden sun will shine for me!

—Lyrics by Douglas Cross and music by George Cory.
—Sung and made famous by Tony Bennett, 1962

The famous little ballad set in a city by the bay, speaks more truly than I ever thought possible. I've since realized maybe a small piece of our hearts was left behind in San Francisco too. We loved this wonderful city, and its capacity to transform. San Francisco can do anything from making public transportation into an exhilarating ride over the city, turning a neighborhood's working class ethic into a home for social revolution, to rehabbing a place of incarceration into an institution of history learned. Wow! We experienced all this in a few summer days which were filled with adventure, fun, laughter, and inspiration. I don't think it gets any better—except possibly with the company kept.

Laura E. Walker

SITES UNSEEN TIPS

LOOK WHERE I'M GOING

I'll say it right up front. Don't assume your sighted guide knows what they're doing. I may be coming across as a tad harsh, but it's your well-being at stake here. Let's reference my attempt to board the cable car with my mother's guidance and my unfortunate head banging. Despite my mother's complete familiarity with my blind status, she has a certain deficit in the ability to guide, mostly because we see one another only a couple of times a year. Taking the time to do a bit of refreshing with guiding techniques would be wise. I neglected to do so and quickly learned of my error. It would even be beneficial to occasionally review with those individuals from whom you normally seek sighted assistance. They get accustomed, sometimes lazy, or simply forgetful. If you ever feel unsafe, it is your responsibility to say so. I have many times stopped and stated I felt we were traveling to fast, I was concerned about obstacles, or whatever it was that bothered me. Your guide is your eyes and must remember are walking for two, but sometimes a simple reminder and review are warranted.

NARRATED TOURS

As you plan your trip and narrow down the sites you want to see, take into consideration what kind of narration takes place on offered tours. Narrated tours can be excellent enhancements to any site seeing venture, but inquire ahead of time to find out how it's done. As with Alcatraz and the bay cruise, the radio broadcasted pre-recorded narrations were amazing. I could clearly hear all being said and the special sound effects made the experience come to life. Quite often tours will utilize public address systems, which can be good if you put yourself in the right place to hear them. Always ask about this when purchasing the tickets and if need be, request to be accommodated in sitting near the speaker. As this particular trip demonstrated, a variety of means to provide narration can be used. I recommend, if you can avoid the bullhorn approach of disseminating information from your guide, do so. It can work, depending on the user, but often you are blasted one second, and then can't hear a thing when they turn. Of course this is dependent on the surrounding conditions, such as moving buses, time of day, and indoor or outdoor venue. Take the time to do the research, inquire, because when you can hear about those images you're not seeing, the story will bring it into view.

THE END

There it is; a few stories about some wonderful American cities as I see them. The opportunities I've had to travel and be with my friends and family are moments I will always cherish, and the chance to recreate them in words has fulfilled a life-long dream. In the midst of this writing process, and while atop my treadmill, a thought poked at my brain and led me off the sweat inducing contraption. A tad more poetic than I am accustomed to from my writing, I thrust it upon you for consideration.

I say this not to put down those who are perfectly ably eyed, not in the least. Matter of fact, more power to them for they allow me the chance to get about, provide information requiring sight, and do a whole host of good with their vision abilities. Rather, I want to strongly make the point that those who may have limited ways of seeing, might just be the best at seeing things the way they should.

I have often referred to my mind's eye and how it has allowed me to make the setting I choose, conjure up the appearance of an individual as I see fit, and generally create things in my own image. My environment is only limited by my imagination; whereas, those having traditional sight do not often look beyond what they see. Therefore, sight can be more impairing than the lack of it.

More than anything, ability is not about the have and have not of vision, it's about attitude, appreciation, and simply getting out there and doing. I hope you recognize by now that this entire story I told was about what people can do;

-from the example of my mother's reluctance about going cross country and joining us for an awesome Frisco frolic, to those who participated in the Gay Games in Chicago,

-to the woman on the train ride home from New York who not only survived the attacks on September 11th, but has found the goodness in others amidst such tragedy,

-to those guys in Boston that started a revolution, which in turn makes this the nifty America we live in today. Now if you so inclined, you could even throw me in as well, to show just what a person willing and wanting to do, can accomplish.

My goodness, I climbed way up on that soapbox of mine, didn't I? Bottom-line now. I hope you enjoyed reading of my adventures and will now get out there and have some of your own.

CPSIA information can be obtained at www.ICGtesting.com
Printed in the USA
BVOW060858120312

284864BV00003B/4/P